The Great Camouflage

The Great Camouflage

Writings of Dissent (1941–1945)

SUZANNE CÉSAIRE

Edited by DANIEL MAXIMIN

Translated by KEITH L. WALKER

WESLEYAN UNIVERSITY PRESS

Middletown, Connecticut

Wesleyan University Press

Middletown CT 06459

www.wesleyan.edu/wespress

French edition © 2009 Éditions du Seuil

First Wesleyan edition published 2012

English translation © 2012 Keith L. Walker

All rights reserved

Manufactured in the United States of America

Designed by Richard Hendel

Typeset in Quadraat by Tseng Information Systems, Inc.

5 4 3 2 1

Wesleyan University Press is a member of the Green Press Initiative.
The paper used in this book meets their minimum requirement for
recycled paper.

Publication of this book is funded by the Beatrice Fox Auerbach Foundation
Fund at the Hartford Foundation for Public Giving.

Library of Congress Cataloguing-in-Publication Data

Césaire, Suzanne, 1915–1966.

[Grand camouflage. English]

The Great camouflage: Writings of Dissent (1941–1945) /

Suzanne Césaire; edited by Daniel Maximin; translated by Keith L. Walker.

   p. cm.

ISBN 978-0-8195-7088-8 (cloth : alk. paper) —

ISBN 978-0-8195-7275-2 (pbk. : alk. paper)

1. Caribbean literature (French) — History and criticism. 2. West Indies,
French — In literature. I. Maximin, Daniel, 1947– II. Title.

PQ3940.C47 2012

844.912 — dc23   2011050012

The excerpts from André Breton cited in this work are from the Oeuvres complètes,
Pléiade edition, 4 volumes, © Gallimard 1988, 1992, 1999, 2008.

   The poem "Ringing the Bells of Chance" quoted in the article "André Breton,
Poet" is excerpted from Paul Éluard's L'Amour, la poésie, © Gallimard, 1966.

   The excerpt from "Negritude" is from "ABCésaire," in Euzhan Palcy's
Aimé Césaire: une parole pour le 21e siècle (Paris: M. Milo, 2006), pp. 57–59.

Contents

Publication of this book is funded by the
BEATRICE FOX AUERBACH FOUNDATION FUND
at the Hartford Foundation for Public Giving.

Translator's Introduction
Suzanne Césaire and the Great Camouflage

It is now urgent
to dare to know oneself,
to dare to confess to oneself what one is,
to dare to ask oneself what one wants to be.

— SUZANNE CÉSAIRE

The Great Camouflage: Writings of Dissent (1941–1945) assembles in one tome the seven articles Suzanne Césaire (1915–1966) wrote for the cultural journal *Tropiques* during the World War II years of the Vichy Regime in France and its territories, among them her beloved natal island of Martinique. The title of the volume is taken from Suzanne Césaire's culminating essay, published in the final issue of *Tropiques*. Each of her seven articles teases out questions emanating from the nodal concept of camouflage, with its attendant phenomena of blindness and imperative for lucidity. In her diagnostic, Césaire grapples with deception, self-deception, the economic slipknot of the post-slavery debt system, political smokescreens, inauthenticity, bad faith, psychological and affective aberration, and cultural zombification. All are caught in the web of "the great camouflage" or, according to her other formula, "the game of hide and seek" of society with itself.

The great camouflage is a trope that deftly captures a tragic reality, history, and drama of the Caribbean. It proliferates with meaning. Suzanne Césaire was profoundly influenced by surrealism, and the sunflower was one of the great surrealist solar floral emblems of the dawning, eclipse, and rebirth of manifold meaning radiating in all directions. Like the surrealist sunflower, *The Great Camouflage* as a title is expansive in its grasp and illumination of the spectrum of intellectual, cultural, and political questions that have confronted and continue to beleaguer the Caribbean and, indeed, the Americas today. Suzanne Césaire marshals historical and anthropological data and examines the role of the arts in revolution, identity formation, and nation-building. Collectively, her essays provide an all-encompassing trans-historical psycho-socio-diagnostic, in particular of the French Antillean condition.

Suzanne Césaire focuses movingly and heroically, but never sentimentally, on the challenges and responsibilities involved in the future of her land and people as well as on the imperative to find alternative weapons of survival:

> This land, ours, can only be what we want it to be . . .
> Surrealism, tightrope of our hope.

Césaire's gaze and critique are inward and outward, Janus-headed, at a crossroads, looking at Euro-American adventurism on the one hand, and on the other, at the tragic dimensions of Caribbean alienation. While her gaze is unflinching and her critique is vehement, her conclusions are lucid and full of understanding and compassion. When she critiques the path of frenzied assimilation to the White world taken by Antilleans after emancipation in 1848, she concludes:

> [T]he Martinican has failed because, unaware of his real nature, he tries to lead a life that is not his own. The gigantic phenomenon of a collective lie, of "pseudomorphosis" . . . How, why, in this people, only yesterday slaves, can there be this fatal misunderstanding? By the most natural of processes, by the instinct-for-self-preservation game . . . And with overwhelming force, a disastrous confusion takes place in his [the Martinican's] mind: "*liberation means assimilation.*"

Over the centuries, Antilleans had endured the degradations of slavery, the humiliations of colonialist ethnography, and the depravities of the Caribbean plantocracy. The period 1941–1945 was a time when Suzanne Césaire and her *Tropiques* associates felt that things could get no worse and that they had nothing further to lose as the shadow of Nazism advanced into the Caribbean with the installation of Pétain's governors, Admiral Robert in Martinique and Admiral Saurin in Guadeloupe. Denunciations, deportations, disappearances, executions, and murders were routine practices under the fascist Pétainist régime. It was imperatively the time for dissent, and especially for dissident thinking. It was an urgent time as she states in the epigraph, a time to dare: "to dare to know oneself, to dare to confess to oneself what one is, to dare to ask oneself what one wants to be."

Throughout her essays, Césaire is perplexed by the willful amnesia, and by the willful blindness or blind-eye of history, by the knowing or conscious suppression and repression of the self, and by the work it takes not to see. As her mind spins around the Caribbean and back and forth through history, she sees more than one great camouflage.

Implicit in Césaire's reading of the Caribbean past is a critique of the Enlightenment. The double standards of the Revolution, the Declaration of the Rights of Man, and the Enlightenment were for her the great camouflage of Gallic humanist values of liberty, equality, fraternity, and solidarity for Europe, which masked policies of enslavement based on the non-homogeneity of the human species, injustice, and a color caste system for the colonial Antillean subjects abroad.

In the twentieth century, the powerfully seductive allure of Nazi/Fascist militarism, weaponry, war games, and ideology was, for her, the great camouflage of brilliant technology masking evil. In her essay "Alain and Esthetics," she notes that "The crowds were taught the victory of intelligence over the world and the submission of the forces of nature to man." In her "Surrealism and Us," Césaire asserts, "From among the powerful war weaponry the modern world now places at our disposal, our audacity has chosen surrealism, which offers the greatest chances for success."

And there was the great camouflage of the Pétainist Vichy

regime's occupation of France and its colonies that occluded the paradox that France at that time was an "occupied occupier," a colonized colonizer.

The great camouflage of geography is fundamental, of location in colonial Martinique, in the French Antilles, in the greater Caribbean. As Suzanne Césaire asserts, one is in "the Tropics," where extravagant tropical vegetal, geological, and human beauty divert attention from the socio-economic and psychological depravations of the region: for some, "paradise, this soft rustling of palms" . . . for others, the hell of grinding poverty.

In art, for her, there was the great camouflage of mimicry parading as authenticity and involving the inscription of the Antillean self into neo-classical/romantic traditions of French-ness, with an attendant erasure of the original Antillean self. The Negritude poets, especially Leon Damas, insisted upon the extent to which imitation, mimicry, or a schooled resemblance only underscored how emphatically the Antillean was not French. For Suzanne Césaire, the state of Antillean artistic production was miserable and symptomatic of a dead-end assimilation and formidable alienation. These issues are at the core of her articles "The Malaise of a Civilization" and "Poetic Destitution," which ends with the imperative "Martinican poetry will be cannibal or it will not be." Surrealism and Negritude converge, for her line is a progression on André Breton's sentence "Beauty will be convulsive or it will not be." Césaire conflates the two messages: art will not be indifferent to human suffering since it is this indifference that has led to colonialism's teleological culmination in Nazism and the present world catastrophe; nor will art leave the spectator indifferent to human suffering, but rather convulsed and moved to action. To be cannibal implies a selective eating of the Other. A cannibalist esthetic was part of the poetic process of questioning the colonial order, and as such constituted a miraculous weapon against discursive reason. It was also an expropriation and redeployment of the image of cannibal imposed by Europe upon the Americas. As an *attitude*, a cannibalist positionality expressed a hunger for originality, emancipation, economic empowerment, and justice through a *strategic and selective* assimilation of the strengths of Afro-Euro-American values and cultures.

Imitative art, misguided politics, and the social climax in the sociology of colored bourgeois capitalist competitiveness and expenditure as freedom, all contributed to the prospering of the new intermediary class: "The race for economic fortune, diplomas, unscrupulous social climbing. A struggle shrunken to the standard of being middle class. The pursuit of monkeyshines. Vanity Fair." . . . "Thus blossoms in the Antilles, this flower of human baseness, the colored bourgeoisie."

While passionately analyzing the facts of the past and assessing the realities of her present with unyielding scrutiny, Césaire's other passions besides are art, love, and especially freedom in all of its modalities. In addition to camouflage, her other overarching concepts in the essays are Africa and us, Negritude, and surrealism and us. Césaire quotes Breton:

> In art as in life, the surrealist cause is the cause itself of freedom. Today more than ever, to draw one's inspiration abstractly from freedom, or to celebrate it in conventional terms, is to do it a disservice. In order to enlighten the world, freedom must make itself flesh and blood and toward that end, must be reflected and recreated in language, in the word.

The surrealist project entailed the radical transformation of the world, the rehabilitation of the self through a poetically rich and revolutionary deployment of language. As Breton states in the First Surrealist Manifesto, "Language has been given to humankind so that it can make a surrealist usage of it." An example of the alchemy of language, the term Negritude—a neologism of recent coinage— was in 1939, at the beginning of the war, a liberating concept of cultural and self-affirmation smelted in, what Suzanne Césaire would designate, the "alembics of suffering." The insult *nègre* became the badge of honor filled with new *attitude* or *negritude* as language was expropriated and valorized by the object of scorn. As René Menil states in *Tropiques*, "We gathered the insults to make diamonds of them . . . We were the children of derision. No one could believe in our rule." In her response to the letter of indictment from naval lieutenant Bayle, head of censure, terminating publication of *Tropiques* and heaping epithets upon the staff, Suzanne Césaire makes a "surrealist usage of language," revalorizing each intended insult.

> Sir,
>
> . . . "*Racists, sectarians, revolutionaries, ingrates and traitors to the fatherland, poisoners of minds,*" *none of these epithets is essentially repugnant to us.* . . .
>
> . . . "Racists," yes. Racism like that of Toussaint Louverture, Claude McKay, and Langston Hughes — against the racism like that of Drumont and Hitler.
>
> As for the rest, expect from us neither a plea, nor vain recriminations, not even debate.
>
> We do not speak the same language.

The ambitions of surrealism and of Negritude continue their convergence. Negritude was the:

> ambition to reorient Black people, to put them back into the struggle for recognition and dignity . . . . It is the re-appropriation of ourselves by ourselves . . . Assimilation, that is the enemy. Alienation, that is the enemy. Consequently, one must re-become, retake possession of ones welfare, of ones values.
>
> . . . this extension through time and projection into eternity, . . . that is negritude . . . It is quite obvious however that the negritude of a West Indian seeking the recovery of his being cannot be exactly the negritude of an African rooted in his

sense of being, who never doubted his identity. These are two very different things. They are two temperaments, two different forms of conditioning . . . Our negritude is humanistic. Our negritude is grounded in history. Our negritude is a blossoming-rooting of possibilities. ("Negritude," *ABCésaire*)

The German ethnologist Leo Frobenius (1873–1938) is the subject of Césaire's first essay. In his *History of African Civilizations*, Frobenius presents cultures as biological or living organisms, as in Ethiopian plant-like or Hamitic animal-like cultures. The fact that his ideas are controversial or outmoded today is not the point. Frobenius's explorations, research, and concepts were crucial portals for the imagination of the Negritude intellectuals, artists, and poets, and a powerful counter, according to Césaire, to the "blind myths" of the European colonialist invention of Africa as barbarous and lacking in technology, culture, and civilization. Moreover for Césaire, Frobenius brought her generation to a realization: "Africa does not mean for us solely an expansion toward the elsewhere, but also a deepening of our knowledge of ourselves." Frobenius's most curious idea is his concept of "Paideuma" or surge-shock-seizure, which is a Manichean—bipolar—force of life and death, good and evil, potential that precipitates transmutation in the human. Such transmutations are economic, social, cultural, epistemic alterations of consciousness and worldview, alterations of, as he calls them, the *sentiment of life*.

For Césaire, Frobenius provides a way of explaining Europe or the Hamitic competitive and technologically driven *homo hierarchicus œconomicus* of the colonial and World War catastrophes. As she states: "This veritable madness for power and domination, which turned humanity upside down during catastrophes as horrible as the wars of 1914 and 1939, is the symptom of a new surge of the Paideuma."

Césaire's analyses reveal a "felicitous encounter" between the esthetics of Emile-Auguste Chartier known as Alain (1868–1951), the French professor-philosopher, and the revolutionary positions of French poet André Breton (1896–1966). They share a belief, a faith even, that "seizing and admiring a new art opens up to the artist unsuspected possibilities however, in the very spectacle of things ignored and silenced."

Negritude and surrealism as art, poetry, and the struggle for total liberation and uncompromising freedom are the access roads away from the sordid reality of inhumanity, inequality, injustice, and war toward an "elsewhere" of reality transformed into a humanistic, egalitarian, all inclusive sur-reality of peace and love re-discovered and re-invented.

Suzanne Césaire and *the warrior heart of hummingbird-woman*

The collateral "pieces" of *The Great Camouflage* provide a multi-faceted almost cubist portrait of Suzanne Césaire from the many perspectives of those who have written so passionately about her and in collaboration with her.

Among the *Tropiques* staff, aside from her husband, René Ménil was perhaps the most kindred of intellectual spirits for Suzanne Césaire. Ménil's cultural critique was uncompromising, and his rhetorical style trenchant. His essay "Let Poetry Go" echoes Suzanne's assessment of the wretched state of Martinican literature in her essay "Poetic Destitution." Each ends with a syntactic variation of "Martinican poetry will be cannibal or it will not be." Moreover, René's "Let Poetry Go" and Suzanne's "The Great Camouflage" contemplate the enigmatic beauty of the tropical forest.

Both René and Suzanne admired Duke Ellington's "marvelous *Mood Indigo*" with, as he noted, its infinitely subtle variations of acoustical tones "between muted and blaring," reminiscent of the nuances of the Antillean dawn and dusk and the floral and arboreal variations in the awe-inspiring and inexhaustibly energizing Absalon tropical forest near the Mount Pélé volcano. For the Césaires, this forest was the privileged site of communion for themselves and with a remarkable circle of writer, artist, and intellectual intimates: the phantasmagorical tropicalist Cuban-French painter Wifredo Lam of "The Jungle"; the painter of "Vegetal delirium," André Masson; the prickly "pope" of surrealism, André Breton, who, enchanted by the couple and by Martinique, wrote "A Great Black Poet" for Aimé, and unabashedly "charmed" by Suzanne's beauty, intelligence, and temperament, wrote "For Madame Césaire." In their "Creole Dialogue" from *Martinique: Snake Charmer*, Masson and Breton sum up the complex emotional and esthetic experience of the Absalon forest:

> We think we can abandon ourselves with impunity to the forest
>   and there all of a sudden its twists and turns obsess us:
>   shall we ever get out of this green labyrinth, shall we not be
>   at the Panic Gates?
> —By a stroke of good fortune we shall not have to search very
>   far for the antidote.
> [The forest, the tropical flowers are] "the heraldic end of
>   the conciliation we seek between the perceptible and the
>   boundless, life and dream—it is through an elaborate gate
>   that we shall pass in order to continue to advance in the
>   only valid way that is: through the fire."

Suzanne died at age fifty from a brain tumor and following a three-year separation—at her request, Maximin points out—from her husband. Ina Césaire, one of their six children—Jacques, Jean-Paul, Francis, Marc, and Michelle were her siblings—provides a tableau of life with "my mother," Suzanne Roussi Césaire, or "Maman Suzy" as the children called her. In reaction to her rigor as a teacher, some students mischievously called Madame Césaire "The Black Panther." The concrete details of Ina's remembrance flesh out the other, more abstract, evocations of Suzanne by Breton, Masson, and Aimé Césaire. Ina recalls her mother's physique, indulgence, temperament, and distinction:

> long graceful silhouette, with the electric hair that she loved to undo to amuse us . . . At the time no other mother smoked and no other mother read Chekhov with her morning coffee . . . My militant mother hungry for freedom . . . alert to every stage of women's liberation. . . . My mother who believed more in struggles than in tears . . . with fragile health, but indefatigable tenacity . . . who was not able to grow old.

In conformity with the surrealist goal of total understanding and the resolution of ancient antinomies, in Aimé Césaire's poems devoted to Suzanne, the high and low, life and death, the perceptible and the boundless, wakefulness and dream, the communicable and the language of Baudelairean "mute things," "cease to be perceived contradictorily," and thus in a poetic bound of ever hopeful reunion overcome the pain of separation:

> Friend
> We shall spread our oceanic sails,
> Toward the lost surge of the pampas and the rocks
> And we shall sing to the low tides
>> inexhaustibly the song of the rising dawn.

The pain nonetheless returns for a lifetime.

The poems for Suzanne by Aimé are dominated by the fusion of sun and water and by phenomena inhabited by the will and power of fire and water: lightning, electricity, plant and floral life, waterfalls, fountains, and the solar flight of hummingbirds. In certain Amerindian cultures, hummingbirds are the souls of dead warriors returned to earth from the sun. The work of the poems is that of transcendence: of life and death, of separation, of this world to another, of the pain of absence that is persistent presence. Shafts of sunlight fill fountains. Sunlight pierces the clouds, which appear to wink. At times, sunlight slashes the clouds, opening a wound of absence and leaving the scar of remembrance. At other times, sun-falls of light or (water) falls of sunlight pour through the azure void, a balm for searching eyes and heavy hearts. Hence Aimé writes for Suzanne:

Through the cicatricial opening-closing games of the sky
I can see her fluttering her eyelids
Just to let me know that she understands my signals
Which are moreover in distress from very old sun-falls of
    light
Hers I truly believe to be the only one capable of capturing
    them still . . .

Returning to the hummingbird image, it is Suzanne herself, in her last article, "The Great Camouflage," who privileges this figure as a key to understanding the intensity, energy, and unfixable iridescence of her complexity as an Antillean.

the hummingbird-women, tropical flower-women, the women
of four races and dozens of bloodlines, they are there no longer
. . . , nor the sunsets unlike any other in the world . . .
Yet they are there.

The passage is rich. It should be observed that the recognition of the interpenetration of indigenous and neo-indigenous bloodlines and cultures—hybridity, métissage, or creoleness—is for Suzanne Césaire neither a new essentialism nor a flight from the fundamental fact and immanent lived condition of blackness in the Antilles and in the world.

The image of the hummingbird traverses her texts, and several of the collateral texts in the volume, as an emblem of fragility, rare beauty, and incomparable stamina. In "Son of Thunder and Lightning," there "at her bosom a bouquet of hummingbirds breaks up." In "Antille," André Masson paints the still point of dynamic immobility of the tiny bird against the swirling verdant chaos of the tropical forest:

Crested with bamboo groves my wild mountain head collides
with a daydream of a nude in the clouds and sees, diving from
a maelstrom of foliage—hovering in its flight—the hummingbird.

Hummingbirds often imagize the transition from the physical
world to the spirit and spiritual world and a beauteous struggle
against adversity, as in Aimé Césaire's *A Season in the Congo*: "the few
drops of dew that make the hummingbird's plumes more beautiful for having traversed the storm." The hummingbird is a self-
abnegating figure of intercession and salvation for humanity. With
twenty heartbeats per second, capable of flying backwards, am-
biguously beautiful and associated with pollination and fecundity,
the hummingbird is a symbol of male and female virility and pene-
tration. Another text by Aimé Césaire, not included in this volume,
condenses the hummingbird iconography as it relates to the person
and life of Suzanne Césaire. Suzanne's courage and tenacity were
exemplary during the very dangerous *Tropiques* Vichy years, exemplary in facing her constitutional fragility, in accepting the challenges of career, motherhood, and marriage, in requesting separation but not divorce, and finally in battling brain cancer. In Aimé
Césaire's *The Tragedy of King Christophe*, the revolutionary king of the
recently liberated Haitian people speaks to his page of battles, impending death, and the warrior heart of the hummingbird:

Yes, Congo. You have, we have, a proverb that says:
"When you see an arrow that's not going to miss you, throw
    out your chest and meet it head on." You hear me? Head on.
Addresses Page directly
Congo, I've often watched
the impetuous hummingbird in the datura blossom
and wondered how so frail a body can hold
that hammering heart without bursting
Africa, rouse my blood with your big horn

Make it open like a giant bird.
Ah, cage of my chest, don't burst.

Suzanne Césaire's seven essays are a fertile intellectual terrain from which have germinated many strains of reflection upon the Antillean predicament: the thought and innovations of the ethno-psychiatrist Frantz Fanon; the theories of camouflage and the rhizomatic or multi-rootedness of Antillean culture elaborated in Édouard Glissant's *Caribbean Discourse*; the critique of the colored bourgeoisie or of Caribbean Bovarysm, initiated by Jean Price-Mars and taken up by Marie Vieux Chauvet, that other neglected female voice from that other French-Caribbean island, Haiti, particularly in her 1968 triptych *Love, Anger, Madness*.

With the publication of her collected essays in French and here in English, it is my hope, shared with the French editor Daniel Maximin, that Suzanne Roussi Césaire's place and importance in the genealogy of Caribbean intellectual thought will be made clearer and that her life and work will emerge from behind *The Great Camouflage*.

KEITH L. WALKER

Translator's Note

Daniel Maximin's *The Great Camouflage* assembles the writings of Suzanne Césaire, poems dedicated to her by Aimé Césaire, texts by André Breton, André Masson, René Ménil, and Ina Césaire as well as Maximin's introduction to the volume. All are accomplished artists with distinct writing styles. The challenge of this translation has been to respect the variety of styles and attempt to render them in English. Suzanne Césaire's style is modern almost modernist: erudite, poetic, at times simultaneously precious and vehement, rhetorically sophisticated, and reasoning often by powerful juxtapositions. Her message is always unambiguously clear. There is a sense of urgency and breathlessness in her style that leads to ellipses and to free-standing phrases or dependent clauses, resulting from the intentional elimination of introductory elements or presentations, the suppression of any unnecessary non-functional grammatical structures, the use of parallel structures, a preference for nouns or nominalization, and the suppression of unnecessary conjunctions, verbs, and predicate forms. If such is the case for Suzanne Césaire, it is all the more densely so for the Guadeloupean poet, novelist, and essayist Maximin, whose style is a syntactically compact, Continental intellectual one with, at times, paragraph-long sentences, delicately balanced with dashes, commas, and colons. The result is the communication of a staggering amount of information with syntactic control and economy. All of the texts bear the mark of surrealism's linguistic experimentation and inventiveness. Translation often unavoidably fixes the explosive proliferating meanings of words from another language in a less than perfect *translatio* or carry-over, and that is the angst and awareness of every conscientious translator.

Suzanne Césaire's seven essays build sequentially toward what might be described as a dissident lyricism. For readers accustomed only to some of the more tantalizing and out-of-context published excerpts or only to translations of the incomparable crescendo of the dissident lyricism of Suzanne Césaire's social and political critique in her culminating essay, "The Great Camouflage," some of the essays that pre-date it might appear uncharacteristically academic. The opening lines are often ponderous, precious, indeed pedantic, by today's standards. Translation aims first and foremost for accuracy, and at times such a goal becomes an archeology. Such a concept might seem ill-applied to texts from the twentieth century, and yet people today neither speak nor write as they did in 1939. Thus translation does become archaeology in its linguistic retrieval or recovery of language as practiced by an exceptional individual who neither spoke nor wrote like anyone else, and of a particular class, here a highly educated New World colonized Black elite breaking out of the straitjacket of Western instruction. Translation as archaeology denotes both the recovery of language and the usage of their linguistic moment, here one of brutal repression in which, at deadly cost, these writers sought to remove—on the one hand, the gag imposed by the centuries-old violence of French colonialism and, on the other, the gag imposed by the immediate daily terror and threat of Hitlerism unleashed in the French Antillean colonies against people of color under the Vichy regime. While there are lyrical moments in the writing, in a time of such crisis one should not expect continuous and languid poesy prose from a writer who, in fact, condemned the dead-end fetishized exoticism and blindness of a poetry of parrot-calls, coppery native bodies, rosy dawns, and iridescent seas, and the empty sonority of endless alliterations and assonances. (See essays "Poetic Destitution" and "Let Poetry Go.") As Césaire's Trinidadian contemporary C. L. R. James asserted in The Black Jacobins concerning certain Caribbean historians, "They wrote so well because they saw so little."

There is a scientific and professorial rigor of presentation and analysis in Suzanne Césaire's essays. The ponderousness of her opening lines was a rhetorical ploy, indeed a camouflage, to divert the attention of the censors away from the dissident consciousness-raising content at the core of the essays. She is laying out her own pedagogy of the oppressed. Her curriculum is not that of Prospero's books but of Caliban's readings by, among others, the anthropologist and Africanist Leo Frobenius, the philosopher esthete Alain, the revolutionary poet and thinker André Breton, and by the writer herself, Suzanne Césaire, the socio-diagnostician.

I dedicate this translation to my brother, to my rock: William "Billy" Walker, Jr.

Editor's Introduction

Suzanne Césaire *sun-filled fountain*

in those days, it was the time of the parasol of a very beautiful woman
with a body of golden corn and cascading hair
in those days the land was dissident
in those days the center of the sun was not exploding [. . .]
in those days rivers perfumed themselves with incandescence
in those days friendship was a pledge
gem from the sun seized in a bound
in those days the chimera was not clandestine
— AIMÉ CÉSAIRE

In those days, that woman's name was Suzanne Césaire, founder with Aimé Césaire—both at that time teachers at the Fort-de-France Schœlcher High School—along with three teacher friends, René Ménil, Aristide Maugée, and Lucie Thésée, of the cultural review *Tropiques* (1941–1945), for which she wrote seven articles that constitute the body of her work, and that are for the first time published here in a separate volume. *Tropiques* was the most important literary review of the Antilles, in spite of its distribution and publication run limited by circumstances—fourteen slight issues published in Martinique—sometimes censored, subsequently shut down, republished in 1943 up until 1945. Aimé Césaire, Suzanne Césaire, and René Ménil are three writers whose thought, writing, and action in a lasting way enlighten the perspective of Antilleans upon their present-day situation.

In those days: it was 1941; Suzanne, born in Martinique in August 1915, was twenty-six years old. She would shortly thereafter have four children—and later six in all—with her husband, the poet Aimé Césaire, then twenty-eight years old. They met during their literature studies, and married July 1937 at the city hall of the nineteenth arrondissement in Paris, Suzanne dressed in a red tailored suit to underscore the secular, blazing, and amorous dimension of their union, and perhaps also as a symbolic reminder of her maiden name, lost that day: Suzanne Roussi.

In those days, her sun-filled beauty and power, visible in the sparkle of her eyes and the radiance of her hair, also revealed a fragility in her vine-like body, rarely still and never rested. A body given to fertile eruptions but devoured by an inner hell—of serious pleurisy that year—saved by a fourth, regenerative, pregnancy. According to her doctor, the space created in her body for her first daughter, born in 1942, preserved her from the ravage within— "windows of the swamp . . . upon the heavy silence of the night"— for two decades of respite, until the sudden irruption of a brain tumor aggressively fatal to her just as she turned fifty.

In those days, the world was in the midst of a war, and the Lesser Antilles, invisible to Hitler, were far from spared by Pétain. It was "the time of Admiral Robert" in Martinique, "the time of Saurin" in Guadeloupe, eras named for the two governors delegated by the Vichy power. They were organizing a "French occupation," imposing fascist order through rapidly issued decrees of purges, internments, deportations to the Guyanese penal colony, and exactions of every kind against the population with the alliance of certain colonialists and the powerful repressive force of hundreds of French naval riflemen who had taken refuge in the Antilles with the help of gold from the Bank of France. To which situation was added the misery occasioned by the Allies' blockade and quasi-autarchy, during which nothing any longer got through from the outside, neither food nor fuel, neither books nor notebooks.

But far from remaining silently subjected, the Antilles rapidly entered into resistance, in the image of the little Haitian state declaring war against Hitler just before the United States had done, with the keen feeling of participating in an anti-fascist international movement, as the inaugural text of the first issue of *Tropiques* in April 1941 announced:

it is no longer time to be a parasite upon the world, it is a matter of saving it. It is time to gird one's loins like a valiant man.
Wherever we look the shadow is advancing. One after the other
the home-fires are going out. The circle of darkness is closing
in, among the cries of men and the howling of wild beasts. Yet
we are among those who say no to the darkness. We know that
the salvation of the world depends upon us also. That the earth
needs each and every one of its sons. Even the humblest.

Those times were the time of "dissidence," a term that would be
used by the powerful Resistance movement in the Antilles to designate the actions of thousands of Antilleans who escaped by canoe
to the neighboring British islands of Dominica and Saint Lucia, to
connect with the Allies and representatives of Free France before
landing in New Jersey. There the gathered Antillean battalions of
Free France (the Free French) embarked on the fight for the liberation of North Africa from Italy, and, ascending the Rhone, until the
liberation of Strasbourg. In the Antilles and in Guyana, internal dissent, resistance, and sabotage and demonstrations of misery and of
dignity combined with pressure from neighboring Anglo-American
allies and with repercussions from certain elements of the Occupation army to lead to liberation in 1943, just two months after the
letter of indictment against *Tropiques*.

In those days, it was Suzanne Césaire who brought the articles
to Admiral Robert's information services for authorization of their
content and to request the necessary paper for printing. The naval
lieutenant receiving her acquiesced to the entirety of the quite pre-
sentable contents proposed: some sparkling lessons for upper-level
classes on Mallarmé, Péguy, Alain, Maeterlinck, Debussy, Lautréamont, favorable to calming the minds of anti-authority students;
some exotic presentations on the African soul or on Hinduism;
some Cuban or Creole animal tales; some scholarly surveys of
tropical plant life and folklore. And especially the omnipresence
of poetry, daily bread without labor, and blessed bread for deflect-

ing the censors' attention from behind the masks of abstract formalism, of botanical precision, of surrealist obscurity, and for the "disordering of all the senses," in which only the distracted and the censors themselves could fail to realize the necessity of reading all of these texts between the lines, especially down to the final line, to be wary of the titles and the harmless openings, in effect explosive time bombs, held impassably in check like the Mount Pélée volcano before the explosion of 1902—texts which, produced for yesterday and reread today, impose, like these seven articles do, the evidence of their actuality, and repeat for every political, economic, or cultural oppressor their major precept: "Accommodate me, I am not accommodating you!"

To fully grasp the context of these nocturnal writings, which over a three-year period, and without too many mishaps, slipped under the boundary line guarded by the censors, we should reread at this point the letter of May 10, 1943, banning Tropiques.

> When Madame requested from me the paper necessary for a new issue of Tropiques, I immediately acquiesced, seeing no objection, quite the contrary, to the publication of a literary review.
>
> I do have, on the contrary, very formal objections to a revolutionary, racial, and sectarian review . . . .
>
> Let us leave aside how shocking it is to see government officials, not only paid by the French state but also having achieved a high level of culture and a first-rank place in society, claim to give the signal for a revolt against a fatherland which has precisely been so very good to them. Let us also leave aside the fact that you are a professor and charged with the mission of educating young people. This in effect does not concern me directly, and let us retain only the fact that you are French.
>
> Excessive centralization is a misfortune from which all French provinces have suffered, coming close to stifling their personality, to substituting it by a conventional and uniform being, to killing art by drying up truth's wellhead. A cold north wind is the symbol of the necessary reaction. I thought I saw in Tropiques the sign of regionalism no

less vigorous and every bit as desirable. I admit I was wrong and that you are in pursuit of a completely different objective. [. . .] As for you, you believe in the power of hate, of revolt, and the goal you have set is the free unleashing of every instinct, of every passion. It is a return to barbarism pure and simple. Schœlcher, whom you invoke, would be quite astonished to see his name and words used for the profit of such a cause.

I therefore forbid the publication of this issue of Tropiques, the manuscript of which you will find here attached.

This time, the very cultivated and usually very tolerant naval lieutenant Bayle, head of censure, had quite clearly understood everything to do with both their goal and their error in judgment: hoping for the Mistral breeze, he found himself lashed by the cyclone of the Césaires. What follows, in this response composed by Suzanne Césaire on behalf of the editorial team, and as Aimé Césaire noted "without her ever having deigned to seduce the jailers," is what the indicted quite willingly confessed to without appealing their conviction,

Sir,

We are in receipt of your indictment against Tropiques.

"Racists, sectarians, revolutionaries, ingrates and traitors to the fatherland, poisoners of minds," none of these epithets is essentially repugnant to us.

"Poisoners of minds" like Racine, according to the Gentleman of Port-Royal.

"Ingrates and traitors to the dear fatherland," like Zola according to the reactionary press.

"Revolutionaries," like Victor Hugo who wrote the "Castigations"

"Sectarians," passionately like Rimbaud and Lautréamont

"Racists," yes. Racism like that of Toussaint Louverture, Claude McKay and Langston Hughes — against the racism like that of Drumont and Hitler.

As for the rest, expect from us neither a plea, nor vain recriminations, not even debate.

We do not speak the same language.

Signed: Aimé Césaire, Suzanne Césaire, Georges Gratiant, Aristide Maugée, René Ménil, Lucie Thésée. Fort-de-France, May 12, 1943.

In those days of deeply entrenched fascism, one could well pay a heavy price for such virulence of provocation. Fortunately, demonstrations and infantry mutinies would point toward the impending denouement of the Occupation, with the victory of dissent two months later, the arrest of Admiral Robert, and the link up with Free France.

One can clearly see in those days, left to themselves, far from attempting to lie forgotten beneath the shadow of their umbrella of paradise, the Antilles lived through a period of great surges of political, social, and cultural dignity. The pride of combating poverty by establishing a subsistence economy and barter system. A bric-a-brac of solidarities in the face of isolation. A legitimate disorder in the face of Pétainist law. A stride forward of internationalist political consciousness in the face of the return of institutional racism (the dismissal of "Black" mayors in favor of handpicked White Creole—*békés*—colonials), while hoping that the defeat of Nazism and the victory of the Allied Forces would lead to the demise of all forms of colonization: colonizers to be dis-alienated in order, according to Suzanne Césaire, to wash away "the stain on the face of France [. . .] of transcending the sordid contemporary antinomies: Whites–Blacks, Europeans–Africans." And at the same time the affirmation of a specificity of identity, which neither the social nor the political up until that point had taken into account: the clear perception of a people standing firmly rooted, what Aimé Césaire was noting in his article "Panorama," published in the reappearance of the review in 1944 after the Liberation:

the worst mistake would be to believe that the Antilles stripped of all powerful political parties are stripped of will power. We know what we want.

Freedom. Dignity. Justice. Christmas up in flames.

One of the elements, the fundamental element of the Antillean malaise, the existence in these islands of a homogeneous block, of a people who for three centuries has searched to express itself and to create [. . .] the Revolution will construct itself in the name of bread, of course, but also in the name of fresh air and of poetry (which amounts to the same thing).

The creative strength of Suzanne Césaire is to have understood very early on the universal dimension at work over three centuries that constructed her Caribbean, the inscription of a history and a geology accommodating to misfortunes as well as to relaxations, to paradises regained as well as to immigrant cataclysms. A geography ultimately rooted in a geology more profound than the arrival of the seasons and a genealogy that recognizes all ancestors without recourse to selective sorting procedures and without the need for roots in order to savor the fruits nor the need of very ancient branches to welcome hummingbirds.

In those days, for Suzanne Césaire it was the most fruitful time of brilliant blossoming, the approximately twenty years covering youthfulness at university, the initial union with Aimé Césaire at the moment of the creation of the *Notebook of a Return to the Native Land*, the Martinique years of creative expression in *Tropiques*, quickly interrupted by their political commitment—Aimé Césaire being simultaneously elected mayor here and deputy representative there, requiring the back and forth, between Paris and Fort-de-France, disruptive of the life of a large family—through the resumption for her of teaching in Paris in order to make ends meet, the "patches of dreams" collapsed, the "sullied foaming wakes," culminating in her decision in 1963 to separate, three years of solitude with no forgetting either for him or for her, "lashed down with heavy hearts," before her swift death in Paris in 1966 and her final return to the soil of her native land.

As with every shooting star, very few people were able to get close to her. But those men and women who did know her well agree on the fundamental importance she had for her entire generation, of which she was the torchbearer, a major inspiration, the mediator of the most profound exchanges. During the '30s and '40s in Paris, she was of that generation of young women conquering the obstacles to freedom and dignity, like their elders the Nardal sisters, who held a musical and literary salon, like her two friends Jenny Alpha, the Martinican actress, and Gerty Archimède, lawyer and great historical figure of Guadeloupe, for which she was the first woman deputy representative in 1945, a position Suzanne Césaire could have taken as well. All three friends luminously beautiful with an inner radiance, bearers naturally of great culture without gloss or glitter, intelligent while distrusting of the strictly cerebral, seductive while refusing to be seductresses, fiancées of Dionysius more than sisters of Eurydice. They took the lead in their dance of ideas and sentiments, choosing more than being chosen, as they would when going dancing with their best male dancer friends, attending the opera or the first Ellington concert, or discussing politics, philosophy, or history over long sleepless nights with their best-friend thinkers of "the holy trinity of Negritude" — Senghor, Césaire, Damas — around favorite subjects: communism, surrealism, poetry of the Harlem Renaissance, Nietzsche and German romanticism, ancient Africa and modern America, without forgetting the place of the love of poetry in poetic creation.

According to her daughters, Suzanne Césaire sang out of tune — without ever denying herself the pleasure of singing — and often. Smoked Royal Navy cigarettes elegantly with a cigarette holder and did not like alcohol, too insufficiently favorable for clear-mindedness and the passion to feel deeply. Adored dancing, contrary to her husband, who in her opinion "had two left feet." Loved to laugh a lot, to keep her hopes up rather than to be polite.

She loved to read outside in nature, for example perhaps Nietzsche and Frobenius, in the sunlight, barefoot, that is to say freely,

unencumbered, alert to the down-to-earth translations of her reading, with self-effacement. For her and her friends heading toward
the decolonization of themselves, two authors were essential, af-
firming like Aimé Césaire: "It is not true that the work of man is
finished." One, Frobenius, making known an Africa from well before colonization, bearer of a system of thought about humankind
as human-plants, as children, rather than masters, of civilization.
The other, Nietzsche, making known a Europe after rationalism
which, so as not to die away at night, must combat the far-too-
human through the fertile fire of transmutations, creators of iden-
tities capable of assuming the multiple through an accommoda-
tion of all possibilities. Wherein she showed to her contemporaries
concerned with rootedness that their Antillean homeland was the
hidden place favorable to the anchoring of such visions and prophe-
cies. As René Ménil would write subsequently in a 1944 issue of
Tropiques: "Antillean romanticism: cultural movement of the Antillean people seized convulsively with the sentiment of its true life
. . . Antillean romanticism resides there and its new conception of
Creole beauty."

In poetry she appreciated that the thoroughly rational *system of
the fine arts* of Alain—who was her professor—places poetry at the
top, although he ignores the loosening of one's control in order to
believe in the "release of ideas." Inversely, she celebrated the art of
diverting every system in order to reach *"the work hidden in the stains"*
through the fertile welcoming of chance and mystery, as in the work
of Breton, who had fascinated them during his stay in 1941, in Martinique, en route to exile in New York, as much as she herself had
fascinated him: "beautiful as the flame of punch." But she could
feel deeply the possible stifling of every creative flame by the poet
of mad love's posture as esthete with, she would say, "his Saint-Just
side," confined in an elsewhere from true life, without the "total
self-effacement" that she postulated for writing to allow itself to be
penetrated by "inner turmoil and abandon."

Beyond these analyses and some dated interpretations one

must imagine Suzanne Césaire happy to conquer her plant-woman Antillean-ness, even from the angle of the bygone concept of "Paideuma" (see her essay on Leo Frobenius). Happy to pen her injunctions to write and to love, for herself, for her love, for her people so Dionysian upon their emergence from the hell of slavery, happy to break with "*doudouisme*"—the sappy folkloric literary tradition—and sentimental spinelessness, with great dosages of love and sexual bamboos. Happy to carry into writing the rhythm of her *anima*, her feminine power, between love and humor in synchronicity with the Nietzschean vision in *The Will to Power*: "There are things that the superior man does not know how to do: to laugh, to play, to dance. To laugh is to affirm life in life, even in suffering, even in the complex. To play is to affirm chance, and from chance, inevitability. To dance is to affirm becoming—destiny—and from becoming, being." For her it is not just about anthropology, it is the question of an ethic, the question of an esthetic, it is a matter of describing oneself as a hereditary daughter without will and testament from this humanity who overcame murderous deracination through the sheer willpower of re-rooting. And through the dance, feet bare throughout.

And it is with Aimé Césaire that, for lack of their dancing together, she breathed a fresh air of poetry, attentive and vigilant to the latter's frenzy of writing, despite the anxiety of his having to write the same thing again, to his refusal to compromise over aesthetic constraints, having mastered so well the mechanisms and the techniques of avoidance that on hundreds of occasions before and after the *Notebook of a Return to the Native Land*, and especially during the *Tropiques* years, he had decided to put an end to it all, to stop writing poetry altogether. A serious physical and mental crisis before the writing of the *Notebook of a Return to the Native Land* and their meeting, a vow to write no more afterwards, were fortunately followed by the powerful creativity of the years of dissent upon return to Martinique, with the long poems "High Noon" and "The Thoroughbreds"; with the first theatrical experience, *And the Dogs*

Were Silent; with the recasting in three or four versions of the *Notebook*, quite different between '39 and '45. And it is she, without a shred of doubt, with all the power of shared love, who in these two great stages of his poetic life made him understand that he could dare to doubt without ever doubting to create, that he had to dare to create as cannibal from the depths of his selfhood.

Well then, one says, why not make herself also a poet-bamboo against poetry-*doudou*? Would it be conceivable that the brilliance of one can cause the other to accept living in shadow? Being caught in the trap by "the pattern of unfulfilled desires." Ultimately, perhaps the secret of the silence so soon to come to pass for Suzanne Césaire means that the cannibal fire of her writings could have consumed her being, her face "of white ash and embers," burning up from its capacity for refusal and commitment body and soul, on the path up to where writing can follow no further. There where *the great camouflage* stops in which all fiction, all poetry, all literature bedecks itself. As in her last text of 1945, which soars well beyond the analysis, the denunciation, the injunction to achieve the most beautiful in style, closest to that of poetry, there where true beings make themselves characters, where logical order becomes confused in staging, where the backdrop of nature transmutes itself into the central character, and there where the woman arrives at the feminine of writing, at the end of her final page, in closing her eyes in order to better perceive the inner night of bodies, of hearts, and of language.

Therein lies the fascinating life lesson of Suzanne Césaire, for in spite of her absolute silence after *Tropiques*—outside of a play, *Youma, Dawn of Freedom*, staged with some of the youth of Fort-de-France, and of which no trace has up until now been found—despite all of the "in spite ofs" that scandalously silence women's writing, in spite of so much space left to man in her life as well as in her texts, in spite of the reticence of poets to liberate their muses, she has, in all her articles here presented, rooted her thought not on a marked-out literary territory, a private property of otherness, but in a land made fertile by all possibilities of writing and a sharp memory. For example, an Africa replanted without nostalgia in the New World and an America assumed, in defiance of all her attributes as woman with "four races and with dozens of bloodlines," and in defiance of all associations. And especially the recognition in her own body, at the heart of the existence her people recovered, reinvented by itself, too overly masked by bourgeois assimilationist decorum, that the Antillean people, whose miracle of calm fervor, turbulent modernity, and such youthful maturity she has powerfully contributed to demonstrating through her far-too-rare writings, remain truly camouflaged behind the deep-down interior of their rebuilt native land.

Yes, in the terrible or reassuring stories invented tirelessly each night for the six children, based on the Creole compost of hunger, trickery, and revolt to be endlessly continued; in the fertile solitude shared with Aimé, each one in oneself for the other; in fervent solidarity toward every true political and poetic commitment without hierarchy, without the pretext of the ivory tower nor compromises of the masses; in the fusion so sensual of bodies into tropical vines and sugary cane in love with the moist embrace of the forests virginal no longer, in the sharp consciousness of a culture of *nurture-by-nature coexistence*, sensitive to the caress of skins soft to the touch, to the offering of breasts that perfume the rivers, in the lucid escort of poets who pass by drunk, blinding themselves with fear that nature will copy them, and in the requirement that esthetics, sensations, and sentiments deeply felt must be tirelessly transmuted into the creation of writing—in all of that is embodied this synthesis of humanity planted, erected into a woman-island of the Antilles: Suzanne Césaire, bright fountain welcoming un-hoped-for "sun-falls of light."

DANIEL MAXIMIN

Part One

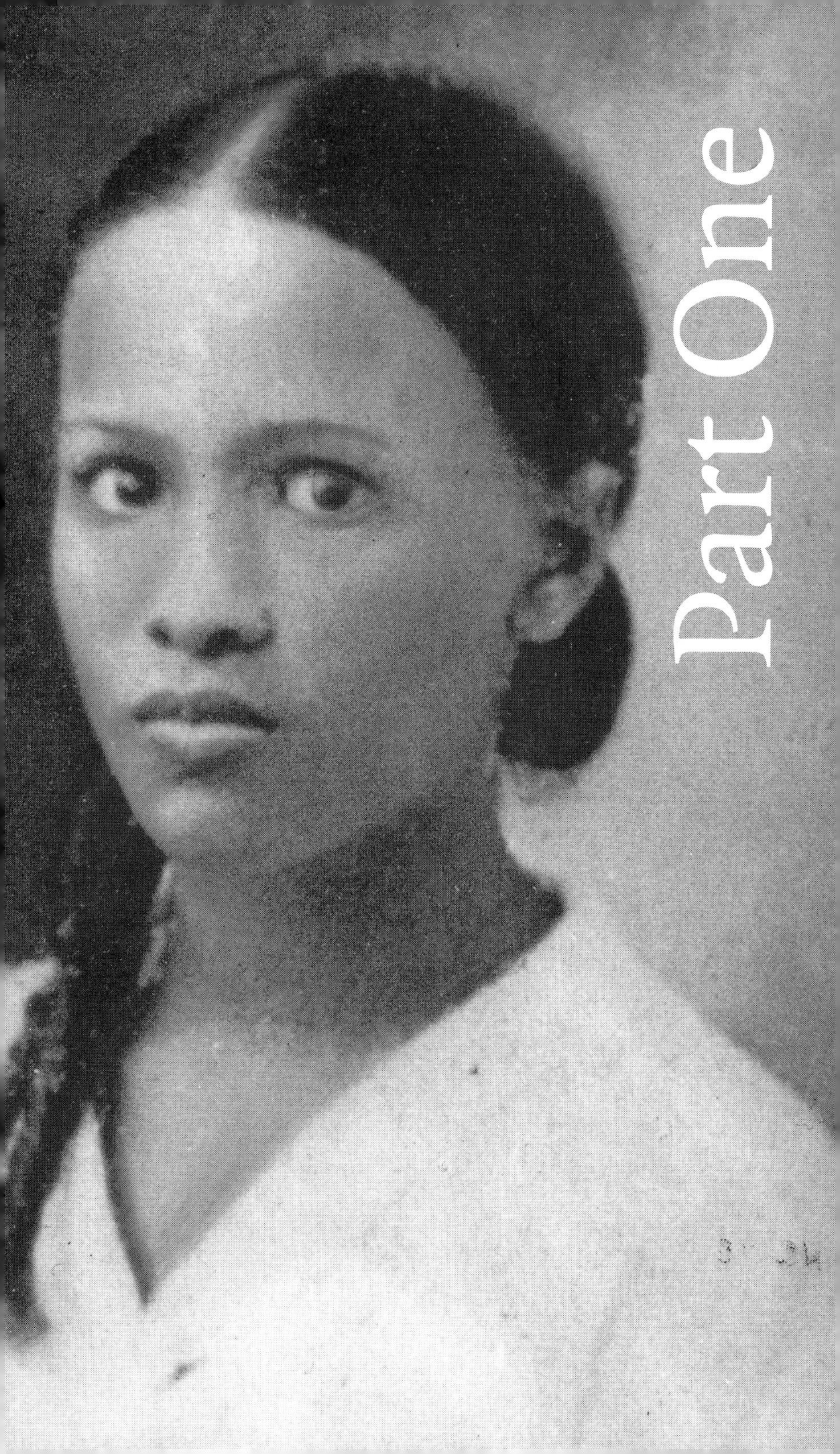

Voum rooh oh
so that times of promise will come back
and the bird who knew my name
and the woman who had a thousand names
of fountain of sun and of tears
and her hair of alevin
and her steps my climates
and her eyes my seasons
and the days without harm
and the nights without displeasure
and the stars of confidence
and the wind of complicity
— AIMÉ CÉSAIRE
   Notebook of a Return to the Native Land, 1939

Leo Frobenius and the
Problem of Civilizations

A fundamental problem is that of civilization. We live it. We celebrate its progress or deplore its decadence. However, what is it in its essence?

Of course at first there are the traditional responses: the humanist response: the work of mankind, done by mankind for mankind; the agnostic response: "a giant organism and we can no more perceive its limits and grandeur than the microbes enclosed in our cells, were they endowed with thought, could perceive the structure and organization of our body."

Those are traditional responses, and then here is a man who knows: historian, archaeologist, ethnologist; indeed one could say: a poet. What is his response? The most extraordinary response possible, the most revolutionary, the weightiest in inferences: No, humankind does not create civilization, no, civilization is not the work of humankind. Quite the contrary, humankind is the instrument of civilization, a simple means of expression of a power which infinitely surpasses his understanding. Man does not act, he is activated, moved by a superior force which pre-dates humanity, a force to be likened to the life force itself, the foundational Paideuma.

And is this Paideuma, creator of civilizations, inaccessible to humankind's understanding? No—humankind truly conscious of its eminent dignity is capable of grasping it, not directly, but its secret is as impenetrable as the secret of the life force itself, but indirectly, in its diverse manifestations throughout humanity. Superior presence, perceptible only to those capable of "seeing in depth."

Let us listen to Frobenius himself: "The Paideuma reveals its specific laws everywhere. Cultures live and die, they are reborn and displace themselves according to particular laws as if humankind were not there, humankind who is only an instrument the Paideuma force makes use of to reveal itself."

The study of the manifestations of the Paideuma life force constitutes a new science that Frobenius calls the Morphology of Cultures. The Morphology of Cultures is neither primitive history, pre-history, nor modern history. It does not accumulate facts or dates. It is not to be confused with archaeology, nor is it ethnology, or ethnography—No. What it seeks is to study "the organic being" of civilization. Civilization itself conceived of as "a metaphysical entity." What it seeks is to grasp beyond the known limits of civilizations, this secret and formidable force that Frobenius names the Paideuma.

A grandiose conceptualization that embraces human evolution in its entirety; an admirable particularity that wants human beings to learn from the study of all other human beings from all other times. Science that is no longer just enlightened order, clever mastery of facts, but the search for intimate knowledge, of a secret reality revealed in the life-force itself.

This enormous effort interests us doubly, because it throws light upon the human problem, and because Leo Frobenius, in order to realize it, devoted himself to the study of African civilizations, and created for himself, as he asserts, an African soul, ways of thinking and feeling that are specifically African.

This study in greater depth of African civilizations, from numerous voyages of exploration, detailed observations of prehistoric rock pictures throughout the African continent and Europe, from comparative observations of religions, morals, customs, habitat, tools, commonly used utensils among most of the Earth's people, here is the abundant material that buttresses the elaboration of a method and a science that marries cold scientific precision with the beautiful daring inventions of the mind.

Leo Frobenius's analytical method moves in two directions:

1. Study of "forms" and of "places": study of the exterior aspects of civilizations, of their distribution in space. One

can thus draw up maps—maps of dwellings on stilts,
for example, during a particular period—one can set up
diagrams, arrive at statistics.

2. Study of "*substances*": this is what belongs exclusively to
Frobenius He says further: "study of the meaning of life"—
he says more precisely: "a civilization, in the sense that we
are giving this word, is not only the outward appearance
of a people, but also the *substance* of an exterior and *internal*
community in which all its members participate.

The first consequence of this method is the observation that the
Paideuma, due to a phenomenon found in all manifestations of the
vital force—the phenomenon of bipolarity—manifests itself literally in two opposite forms: (1) Ethiopian civilization and (2) Hamitic
civilization. Ethiopian civilization is tied to the plant, to the vegetative cycle.

It is dreamy, drawn inward upon itself, mystical. The Ethiopian
does not seek to understand phenomena—to grasp and dominate
facts outside of himself. He lives and lets live, in a life identical
to that of the plant, confident in the continuity of life: germinate,
grow, flower, bear fruit, and the cycle starts all over again. The lived
fact of poetry, felt so profoundly that the Ethiopian is almost never
capable of projecting, of expressing outwardly. Also, for the Ethiopian, the notion of the father, of paternal relations, is fundamental.
To sum up: "The Ethiopian feeling of life defines itself as a sense of
the real and as primitive mysticism." The Hamitic civilization, on
the contrary, is tied to the animal, to the conquest of the right to
live through violent struggle and conquest. The Hamitic is active,
conscious of external occurrences to which he opposes himself and
that he must vanquish in order to survive. He never abandons himself freely to things but strives to dominate them by force or by
magical practices. He does not have the sense of the continuity of
generations, but of individual life. The mother is not required to be
faithful to her husband if he is vanquished in battle. She becomes

the wife of the victor. Briefly, "the Hamitic civilization is character-
ized by the significance of the event and primitive magic."

These two fundamental expressions of the Paideuma can no
longer be found except buried deep in the consciousness of the
peoples of the so-called higher civilizations of Europe, Asia, and
America. On the contrary, in Africa, these forms of civilization can
be studied in an almost pure state among so-called primitive populations. There are some among them who survive in their original,
spectacular simplicity, human-plant, human-animal.

It suffices to interpret, for example, the strange rites of the forest populations where harvesting becomes a religious act, or still
further to recover the original meaning of the cruelties of adoles-
cent initiation rites among most Hamites. The geographic position and the massive form of the African continent have allowed
the preservation of, in so to speak complete isolation, the forms
of civilizations spontaneously sprung up from the soil; it is here
that the alteration, or rather the inevitable evolution, was accomplished more slowly than elsewhere or, one should say, more "in
depth," giving rise moreover in certain parts of the African territory
to civilizations as brilliant as the Gao Empire at a time when Europe
was covered with impenetrable forests and swamps.

From his first voyage to Africa in 1904, Leo Frobenius admired
this remnant of a very ancient greatness. He admired "the gestures,
the mannerisms, the customs . . . with a meticulous attention to
detail, a dignity, and a grace all natural." And he says: "I know
no other people of the North who can compare themselves to the
primitive peoples in terms of coherence of civilization."

Frobenius's *History of African Civilization* is a vast effort of synthesis toward the understanding of all these very ancient forms of
civilization that today appear primitive and frozen in time, whereas
in reality, they are very often symbols of an astonishing richness
and complexity of spectacular cultures of which we know nothing.

Moreover, to the one who poses the harrowing question of
human evolution, the gift of Africa appears invaluable: "Africa does

not mean for us solely an expansion toward the elsewhere, but also a deepening of our knowledge of ourselves."

■

It is thus for Leo Frobenius and his disciples that the comparative study of civilizations is not only the clarification of what it means to be human, but also a glimpse of the future, thanks to the results of the new science. They believe themselves authorized to offer solutions to questions as compelling as these: "the role of the human" and the "drama of the Earth" . . .

In effect Frobenius discovered that the idea of uninterrupted progress, cherished by the nineteenth century, which showed civilization progressing along a single line from primitive barbarism to modern high culture, was a false idea. Humanity does not have a will to achieve perfection. Moreover, it does not create for itself a civilization that aspires to ever-higher levels. It goes forth, on the contrary, motivated by the internal Paideuma, in multiple directions, from one "shock" to the next, just as the vital force goes from mutation to mutation among the diversity of living species. But before specifying this new notion of "shock," it is indispensable that we reveal how the vital force is itself expressed in the Paideuma, creator of civilizations. First of all, the fundamental polarity, sign of life itself, and which we have seen manifested already in the grand Ethiopian–Hamitic opposition: we find it in the details of the life of cultures.

For example, the stars (the moon, Sun, Venus, etc.) find themselves attributed a sex. And the determination of this sexual identity is not arbitrary. It responds to a precise spatial order. The paired stars, twins, brother, sister, lovers reign over particular regions, spread out, according to rules established by card games. Similarly, numbers participate in determining masculine and feminine nature. Thus, the number 4 is tied to space, to movement, to the masculine; the number 3 is tied to time, past, present, future; to the phases of the moon with its birth, its waxing and waning; into repose, into the feminine.

A conjunction charged with meaning, the symbolism of numbers is the reflection itself of the symbolism of the stars, the one and the other the profound expression of the space, time, primitive polarity of the reality of life. Now let us study the psychological process of the "shocks," how the numbers, the stars, the seasons have delivered to humans what Leo Frobenius calls their "essence." How the numbers, the stars, the seasons have determined in plant-man, animal-man a "revolution of the mind," a veritable alteration of his nature that is the distinguishing feature of the "shock."

The phases of the moon, the transit of the sun, the change of the seasons have not been the object of methodical observations on the part of the human who has not sought to draw lessons from these phenomena.

No. Abruptly, man was "shocked" by the essence of these phenomena, by their intimate, secret reality. He was turned upside down by a sudden emotion, urgent and irresistible. Thus the appearance and disappearance of the moon gave rise to the seizure of the concepts of time and death. It is this sudden awareness that is expressed for example in a great number of civilizations by all the rituals tied to the theme of the predetermination of the death of a god. Similarly sunlight illuminating the world gives rise to the grasp of space, of spatial limitation, of delimited order.

When the change of seasons unleashed the sudden awareness of the periodic rhythms of the life and death of nature, a new "sentiment of life" was born. Man became conscious of his individual existence and the problem of his destiny. One can say that at that moment the consciousness of man himself as an isolated reality in the external world was born.

We must not believe that these "seizures, shocks" have been successive stages: plant, animal, star, season have created and changed the nature of the sentiment of life in different places, in different epochs, have truly created and changed civilizations that over here go forth making themselves more profound, over there altering themselves, elsewhere intermingling further, bound the ones to the others in a more and ever greater complexity.

And as well there is how Leo Frobenius arrives at his vision of the future, for he is authorized to now write: "The history of human civilization is the history of the transformations of the sentiment of life." He can now search to see whether in our time a new sentiment is not manifesting itself, if our sad time is not perhaps the explosion of a new meaning, a new awareness, a new sentiment of life.

It seems that Euro-American man in the nineteenth century has been seized with a veritable madness for science, technology, machines, the result of which has been the creative imperialist thought of the world economy and its encircling of the globe. This veritable madness for power and domination, which turned humanity upside down during catastrophes as horrible as the wars of 1914 and 1939, is the symptom of a new surge of the Paideuma. These are surges we cannot fully comprehend, the real meaning of which still remains hidden. Therein lies the drama of the earth. As for the role of humankind, it is to prepare itself for living this other future, it is to allow itself to be moved by the Real, without losing this sense of sacredness, this sense of conquest, this sense of destiny that is its inestimable and unique heritage.

■

There you have the great message of Leo Frobenius to humankind today. His philosophy goes beyond the schoolish reasoning of his predecessors and of his contemporaries. He gave life and power to sociology. He rediscovers the meaning of cosmogonies and myths lost since the time of Anaxagore and Plato.

And this Philosophy is Poetry, the world recreated, humankind master of a new fate, strengthened by a new experience of life. The fruitfulness of this admirable doctrine is that it poses to each of us the immediate problems from which it is impossible to shy away without cowardice. It is now vital to dare to know oneself, to dare to confess to oneself what one is, to dare to ask oneself what one wants to be. Here, also, people are born, live, and die. Here also, the entire drama is played out.

"It is time to gird one's loins like a valiant man."

SUZANNE CÉSAIRE
Tropiques no. 1, 1941

Alain and Esthetics

A peculiar fate is that of Emile-Auguste Chartier, known as Alain.

Political scientist, economist, moralist . . .

His politics read as *defeat*, his "economics" read as *crisis*, and in the face of events that monstrously disrupt the world at this time, his doctrine—pills of optimism—can seem to us a parody.

So what?

Well, it will remain nonetheless that this "professor," this philosopher by profession, will have forcefully laid out the problem of art; will have understood the importance of the extraordinary phenomenon that constitutes poetic creation, and will have consigned it to its proper place: first place! First place in a ruinously extravagant world of bankruptcy, and fraud; first place in a world in which the most dismal of games is being played: the hide-and-seek of humankind and with itself.

It is a mind of exceptional logic and clarity. Alain thinks above all about a system of the fine arts.

And foremost there is a methodical analysis of the arts.

What is drawing, painting, architecture, sculpture?

What is music? Poetry?

The history of art, from drawing to poetry, is for Alain the history of a conquest: the conquest of the human over a set of resistant, stubborn yet manageable forces that we call nature.

And here we are, at the threshold of art, the human alone, almost detached from the obstacle. And it is in drawing that we find artistic expression in a face-to-face conversation with itself.

"No effort, no passion to conquer . . . The hand is light, impartial, indifferent as in thinking." Here, hostile nature hardly opposes itself to artistic expression. Once again drawing is finesse, lightness, freedom, and independence.

More filled with pathos, however, is the combat the painter must wage. Whereas drawing provides us, through a bold and definite stroke, a unique "instant" of the model, painting has as its mission to give us "far more than the instant, the moment, and through this moment, the story of an entire existence." If the point of the strictly pictorial process is thus to stop time, this definition, in its natural implications, leads to this beautiful and exciting idea, one which surpasses the ambition of realizing a lifelike portrait: painting is the expression of total emotion, of life in its completeness. And from that point on, it is easy to see that painting is struggle. First of all, struggle between the painter and time, for it is a question, in an extraordinary effort of synthesis and reconstruction, of finding "the first appearance, the youthful appearance, and like that at the moment of the birth of a world."

Struggle, next, with color that is resistant matter, difficult to handle, difficult to discipline, to harmonize.

This patience of the painter, these difficulties are the condition itself of the beautiful in painting. The painter, through a slow process of strokes and touch-ups, manages to express life—life which itself is also slowness and patience, reversals, accumulations, and changes.

Struggle against time, struggle against matter, such therefore is painting: confrontation of man and the world, the obstacle subdued, victory!

And one could say the same of sculpture and about architecture . . .

Sculpture? Attack unleashed upon the stone, upon the wood that clasps in its arms and imprisons the subject. For let us not be deceived, the subject is not discreet and secret within the artist's thought. It is completely embedded in the material to be sculpted "which seems threatening and smiling, and at first appears to be the head of a man, a horse, a wild boar . . . It is the challenge of freeing it." And in this deliverance, the sculptor, like the painter, dominates not only the matter, but also time. Time, which expresses itself here through movement, for the statue, offered for our contemplation, is beautiful not just in its immobility. Whereby we see the natural progression from drawing to architecture, in the passage from the mobile to the immobile. If line in drawing expresses the moment and pure movement, already in painting, color restricts movement and fixes time.

In sculpture, movement and time are as united, concentrated. For movement is there, irresistible, poised to spring up, but it does not spring up at all.

The immobility of a beautiful statue is full of restrained forces and ideas.

And it is thus that we arrive at architecture in which the immobile reigns. Here is the brilliant triumph of the human.

Thanks to the monument, the human can measure his power. The great natural forces are raised against the architect: wood, stone, steel, weight, and balance, the climates and seasons. But he erects against the sky an imposing witness, like "a second form of nature, more solid, more faithful, better defined."

This is the spectacle offered by the indestructible pyramids.

In the same way, the obvious triumph of man over time.

And the architectural mass in its powerful serenity resists the wave that sweeps away civilizations and empires.

Let us move on now to another art group: music and poetry. Here again the artist struggles, at first against a resistance in some way material. Music must overcome noise. Poetry must conquer the word, which strengthened by the rules of prosody becomes as resistant as marble.

And here is now the definitive victory of the artist, and the most beautiful: the musician, the poet, going beyond the world itself and recovering themselves in a moving confrontation, are each struggling against their own self and dominating it. For Alain, it is there that the secret of beauty in poetic and musical expression resides: music and poetry deliver man from himself and from the excess of his passions.

Melody, for example, quite in conformity with the natural process of every human emotion, its birth, its full expression and its decline, in a way saves the human's dignity, by mastering this emotion.

Beautiful music is the sign of self-control.

As for poetry, it elevates man to the highest degree possible of contemplation and majesty. What is the role of poetry? Like music, it helps us to move beyond ourselves, and it goes yet further, it leads us into "a new time," into a new world. The true and real poem, which shows us the human in terror, in despair, and in horror even, must pull us out of these hells and lead us to mysterious beaches of consolation. The pain, once expressed, is dominated. The words, assembled following the rhythm, have vanquished the unhappiness. Poetry, more so than music and more serenely, is the expression of a kind of happiness, born of a feeling of deliverance.

■

Here then is the beauty born of the effort, from the struggle, from the most dramatic of confrontations, that of the human with the self.

And here it is now, through an *astonishing contradiction*, expressing harmony, peace, and union. Art is no longer the sign of a struggle and a victory, but the sign of an entente between the artist and the artistic material. This is visible in sculpture where the artist allies himself with the wood, for example, with its knots, its flaws. Then the work is made much more from intelligent collaboration than from brutal violence. Contradiction!

Likewise, the same is true for architecture: a beautiful edifice is the sign of an accord between the material and the mind. The historic monument bears witness to the value of this pact by its survival, its solidity, its imposing mass, and its harmonious lines: the ancient aqueducts, in their beauty, are "arcs of alliance—arches of alliance" for Alain, because they are witnesses to the geometric law that is derived from the mind as much as from nature.

Art is therefore "felicitous encounter," harmony, peace. The search for artistic expression suddenly appears supple and nuanced, and is accompanied by joy. It is a matter of harmonizing nature's power with the power of the mind. "This point of felicitous obedience," Alain states further, is the difficult goal to achieve in all the arts. Nature is no longer adversarial and intimidating, it is on the contrary friendly and inviting to the artist; it is accommodating, better for him than for his own self. And musical emotion also finds its bearings in the degree of peace and happiness that it provides, in the degree of balance and harmony it introduces into the imbalance of the passions.

More than any of the other artists, the poet abandons himself to nature. He has confidence in it. And it is along this path of confidence and abandon that he attains success and grandeur. Contained in his own human nature, there is the reflection of universal nature, a meeting point, a place of balance that it is a question of determining. So the poet has encountered truth, the truth of the world and of himself. It is thus that poetic beauty is born. Alain goes still further. He declares that beauty is not truly expressed until the "encounter" has surpassed the expectations of the artist.

"The day when what one wanted to do finds itself surpassed by what one has done, then there is beauty."

This idea opens up to artistic expression unsuspected paths from Alain himself, and quite extraordinary ones.

But here is, drawn from the system of fine arts, the fundamental contradiction upon which, without the knowledge of the author, it rests: "Everything in beauty is spontaneous and at the same time carefully chosen."

On the one hand there is the human, sure of itself, conscious of itself and of its essential difference, struggling, subjecting the world to its choice.

On the other hand there is humankind abandoned, delivered up to these unknowable forces of the world, searching in artistic expression for the happiness of being in harmony with them, the joy of a felicitous encounter. Contradiction! Fundamental contradiction!

■

Thus now does Alain appear to us, caught in the trap, lost on the multiple and secret paths of the arts. The mystery of artistic expression has resisted his masterful analyses. And there he is who confesses his failure before the strangest phenomenon there is, the artistic phenomenon.

Where does art's resistance to complete analysis come from?

First of all from what Alain seeks to understand, to classify, to make clear for the mind alone, that which is not a matter of intelligence, but of feeling and sensation. He gives us the exterior rules of beauty. He defines it. And even if, in front of a beautiful work of art, he has experienced this rush of emotion, this thrill of beauty, he remains singularly reserved, as if full of a secret shame. When, in spite of himself, the emotion breaks through, then the release of ideas in their manifold developments appears to overwhelm him.

He told us that painting had the potential to express all of life. But what then is this life-totality?

Did he glorify the spontaneous in artistic expression? But how far does this abandonment to the creative force go? And what is it, this mysterious, hidden, and irresistible force?

Alain could not venture onto these slippery terrains without true boldness, without enthusiasm, rushes of the heart, surges of passion. These failings have singularly limited his undertaking. For example, the greatest poet for him is Paul Valéry. And he does not feel that the classicism of Valéry can be surpassed, nor that it is outmoded.

For example he defines musical beauty admirably: "music threatened, lost, saved and once again threatened, is the essence itself of music," and he does not know whether his sentence even expresses the process of red-hot jazz.

But let us leave our guide there . . .

It can no longer be a question of those narrow and well-known paths where traditional beauty is offered up in its clarity and obviousness to the admiration of crowds. To these crowds one taught the victory of intelligence over the world, and submission of the forces of nature to the human.

Now it is a matter of seizing and admiring a new art, which while leaving man in his true place—fragile and dependent—opens up to the artist unsuspected possibilities however, in the very spectacle of things ignored and silenced.

And here we are in the realm of the strange, of the marvelous, and the fantastic, which people of certain taste hold in contempt. There is the liberated, dazzling, and pleasing image of a beauty that is precisely the most unexpected, the most upsetting. There we have the poet, the painter, to preside over these metamorphoses and these wrenching twists of the world under the sign of hallucination and madness. Here they are abandoning themselves to all the obscure and unknown forces of their being, and in a vertiginous descent into hell, of which there exist testimonies that are pure masterpieces. Allow one to think about the works of poets like Rimbaud and Lautréamont. Here finally is the world, nature, things entering into direct contact with the human who has recovered spontaneity, the natural, in the fullest sense of that term. Here finally are the veritable communion and the veritable knowledge, chance overcome, recognized, mystery friendly and helpful.

And here, it is appropriate to cite the name of André Breton, his poems, his admirable book: Mad Love.

Through a curious encounter, Alain in his System of the Fine Arts and Breton in his Mad Love propose the same example to the reader: Da Vinci advising his students to create a coherent painting from the contemplation of stains on an old wall. The distance that separates the two men is measured by the extreme difference in interpretation of this lesson from Da Vinci. Alain, the philosopher by profession, sees therein the obvious proof that art is above all technique and practical experience, patience, choice, since the subject hidden in the stains can be made to emerge merely by dint of treatments and touch-ups. Breton, the authentic poet, himself declares that Da Vinci has resolved here the great philosophical problem of the relationships of the human and the world. Here in effect, the hidden work in the stains is a response of the thing to the artist, a response that is a projection of the secret self of the artist, of his "desire," a response that is also the voice of the unknown and of mystery. The work of art appears, then, as the sign of the veritable alliance between the thing and the human. And this alliance cannot have its full and complete meaning unless the artist, in a voluntary abandoning and total relinquishing of the self, steps back, a certain way, so that the mysterious message can burst through. In poetry, it is, for example, the triumph of automatic writing. At any rate in all the arts, the old horizon withdraws and broadens beyond the conceivable. The most beautiful ambition of the human is realized: to know the unknowable. Art is the only, current, access road toward this other enticing world. Such is the power that is delegated to the artist. We are entitled to expect the artist to perform miracles.

Here therefore are defined the immense paths of the new art, which is opposed to the narrow and classical conceptions of official critics. A splendid new interplay responds to a new consciousness of the world, to a new consciousness of the human. And already some unsettling masterpieces are evidence of this recognition, and here now rise upon this world, transfigured and recovered, the promises of an art that will be the total expression of life.

SUZANNE CÉSAIRE
Tropiques, no. 2, July 1941

André Breton, Poet

The poetry of Breton is decidedly one of happiness! While ignoring in no way the sufferings and maledictions that fill the dreams of Baudelaire and Rimbaud with horror, it is a poetry which overcomes and resolves them. For if like Rimbaud, Breton is a "seer," he does not allow himself to be hypnotized by the dreadful dreams of Rimbaud's hell. Amidst horror and anguish even, Breton knows how to detect the subterranean mesas of joy. Despair? But this despair "enchants him." His life? The most serious problem! But he knows to attach no importance to life. And for him death is "rose colored," and here under his sharp gaze, the multiple aspects of life, all the contradictions, all the mysteries are clarified.

Supreme reward of the supreme science that is poetry.

And in effect Breton inhabits a marvelous country where clouds and stars, winds and swamps, trees and animals, humankind and the universe yield to his desires.

It is a familiar and yet fantastic country where all things communicate through signs. And Breton responds to these signs. And here we are, introduced by him into the very heart of this country, vaster, richer, more beautiful, more true, where, beyond consciousness, our most troubling daydreams flower.

Here, in a moving and sensitive existence, lived monsters and flowers that ravished our childhood with fright: wise birds, winged squid, sea anemones. Here "cats curling up upon themselves have formed chimneys upon rooftops." Here "giant lilies twist around their own waists and the bloody mannequin leaps on three feet in the attic."

In this wondrous world, telegraph wires are enchanted, grass is electric.

And we are not surprised to hear within ourselves ". . . the sighs of the glass statue that sits up on its elbow when man sleeps, and in his bed bright gaps open up."

Gaps through which one can glimpse "stags in a clearing in coral woods and nude women at the bottom of a mine."

Who will doubt the reality of these visions?

Already within us, outside of ourselves, the most unexpected, the most disquieting metamorphoses are taking place. Objects and beings no longer have defined shape, and time no longer exists.

And now the marvel of all marvels: love.

"Human love," Breton writes in *Communicating Vessels*, "is to be redefined like all the rest. I mean that it *can*, that it must be re-established upon its true foundations."

Love, beyond all conventions, reclaims its place among the great elemental forces: Love, Mad Love. For it is—

the unutterable-without-oath reign of the crackling
Nameless Woman
Who splinters the jewel of the day into a thousand shards.

This strange hymn for the woman, this convulsive call to the powers of the world and of desire, where love takes its full meaning, which is to integrate the human with the cosmos, placed in direct contact with the elements.

My wife with hair of wood burning fire
With thoughts lightning strikes of heat
With the hourglass figure
My wife with the dimensions of an otter clenched between
    the teeth of a tiger
With arms of sea-foam and floodgates
and with the blend of wheat and mill
My wife with legs of rocket flares
With movements of clockwork precision and despair
With eyes at water level, air, earth and fire level.

And this other couplet from *Mad Love*—one of the purest summits of French lyricism:

"Nature is subject to flare up and to snuff out, to serve and not to serve me, only to the extent or to the moment where rise and fall for me the flames of a hearth which is love, the only love, the love for another human being. I have known, in the absence of this love, skies truly empty, the flotsam of everything I was about to grasp on the Dead Sea, in the desert of flowers. Was nature betraying me? No, I felt that the principle of its devastation was in me.

The only thing missing was a great iris of fire emerging from me to give some value to what exists. How beautiful everything becomes in the light of the flames! The most insignificant shard of glass finds a way of being simultaneously blue and pink. From the upper heights of Mount Teide, Tenerife, where the eye can no longer see the slightest blade of grass, where everything could be so frozen and so somber, I contemplate to the point of dizziness your open hands above the now-blazing fire of twigs we just kindled, your enchanting hands, your transparent hands gliding over the fire of my life."

◼

What Breton delivers in this way, in this poetic profusion, is the secret multiplicity of his desires, his real self, that self suddenly intoxicated to know itself, surprising itself with its own freedom.

Too much freedom was given to me all at once, freedom to make those I miss live again, freedom to pursue the apparitions standing real before me.

In effect it was about rediscovering divine freedom, the divine power of dreams and of childhood.

Let us reread the Surrealist Manifesto:

The mind that plunges into surrealism relives with exaltation the best part of its childhood. It is perhaps childhood that comes closest to one's true life. Childhood beyond which man has at his disposal, aside from his free pass, only a few complimentary tickets; childhood where everything conspires to bring about the effective and risk-free possession of oneself. Thanks to surrealism, it seems that these chances come back once again.

And from that point when time is abolished, when the past, the present, the future are merged, when we live this unique state which permits us to recapture plenitude and that sense of the moment which thrills us so in young children so similar, as they are, to cats, dogs, calves, butterflies, flowers, and sand—can we not reasonably speak of freedom?

Freedom to do and to undo—that which Breton defines in the second manifesto of surrealism: "A poem must be a collapse of the intellect . . . After the breakdown everything begins anew—sand, oxyhydrogen blowpipes."

And the freedom that Éluard sings of:

Ringing at full peal all the bells of chance
They played at throwing cards out the window
The winner's desires took the horizon's shape
In the foliage of deliverances.
He burned the roots the summits disappeared
He broke the barriers of the sun the ponds
In nocturnal plains the fire sought the dawn
He began all voyages at the end
And on all the roads
And the earth in losing itself became new.

Abysses of the unconscious. Abysses of the marvelous. Freedom that other abyss. André Breton asks no more of life than to frequent them.

Abyss, gathering of the glimmering insights that I do not have
Enormous pearls
Unmapped abysses that draw me in

I am handcuffed when I think of you
And yet, I am free to lose myself in you.
To maintain with that which emerges from you the least
   collaborative of exchanges.

But also from frequenting abysses, what magnificent reward! The poet becomes a prophet.

Infinite roads, along which the mind arrives at a more and more secure grasp of the world.

Roads of yesterday and tomorrow where the mind renews forgotten ties with the diversity of the world. Bright clear roads where humankind, freed from the bonds of time and space, might *see* clearly, clearly into a past that is at the same time its future—clear in the outward signs that are in complicity with his desires, clear in the daydreams—which are at the same time actions of the day before: total knowledge.

"Prophet with silvery temples purer than mirrors," is this not how André Breton defines himself? And how can one fly in the face of evident talent when the poet recounts in *Mad Love* this marvelous encounter between the defining event of his life and a poem written some ten years earlier? A poem "dictated" by the unconscious and clairvoyant self and whose obscurity makes itself all of a sudden luminously clear.

And similarly the emotion of finding in the "letter to seers" written in 1925 this disturbing phrase: "There are people who claim that war has taught them something. They nevertheless are less advanced than I who know what the year 1939 has in store for me."

Do not allow the theoretician to make us forget the poet.

At the same moment he is the originator of the most extraordinary revolution that ever was, since it also involves not just art, but our life in all its entirety, André Breton is the most authentic French poet of our time. Some have preferred others to him, "prettier," "nicer," more traditional, and all things considered, more cowardly. What does it matter!

The least talented hack among the men of letters will endure as much as the richest.

Supremely indifferent:

I am not on this earth with all my heart.

Supremely "vigilant" and "erudite"

I touch only the heart of things,
I hold the thread . . .

In him there is the exaltation of the search, the marvel of discoveries, the smiling calm of one who knows, the assurance of one who sees.

André Breton, the *richest*, the *purest*.
Blocks of crystal stacked high.

SUZANNE CÉSAIRE
Tropiques, no. 3, October 1941

Poetic Destitution

Martinicans have not forgotten him.
No one has described our landscapes more amorously
No one has sung more sincerely of the "charm" of Creole life.
Languor, sweetness—affectations too—Saint Pierre, the
volcano,
"mornings like blue satin" "lavender evenings."

Adorned in flares, in emerald and red sun
Winged djinns and dwarfs peck at bananas
Which are candies heavy with ambrosia
And all the air was heavy with ambrosia under the lasso
Of long and flexuous jungle vines.

And still more this sonnet that will delight imbeciles:

The clear and floral sky, aware that it is ravishing,
vault of rosy crystal tinkling at the chiming of the bells,
Shimmers, luminous and sweet: at the foot of the rocks —
the black ones dropping off into the rosy waves turning blue,

Fronds quiver in the tamarind trees:
Clear-throated birds warble triple semiquavers,
Stout cabbage-trees release embroidered skeins of feathers
The mother-of-pearlescent Morning dissolves into sapphire.

Good Blacks cast upon the water like ever so many flies
Dark swarm cheerful amidst sudden skirmishes
Mock the bobbing of the long pointed canoes.

The Conch horn with guttural callings of the wild beast
And fishermen lost in the blue ocean spray
Intently watch, heart panged, volcanic peaks of mauve fade
away.

That is called *Antillean Dawn*. And that started a trend.

Naturally.

See So-and-so. And So-and-so. And So-on-and-so-forth. All "Martinican bards."

Any talent? Of course, for people interested in that sort of thing. But what a pity!

He misses the point. He looks. But he has not "seen."

He manages to "pity" the Black. But he has not experienced the Black soul.

Under the somber pecan trees mirrored
In the vitreous water of the bayous bordered with shacks
Lily, were you the little dark child from the South
Of a shiny Black man, almost golden from so much shining,
Black sun with a white sun for a smile?
Were you the tiny prey hunted down, forced
By old hunters hairy, obscene and White,
The favorite quarry, cajoled, then beaten,
The exciting doll soon to be broken
Which they tucked away one evening, poor slender thing,
Near a swamp of jade where tree frogs were singing
Under the grimacing moon?

And he evokes the mountains:

Oh the white laughter of the mountains
In the fragrant night of vegetations,
The languid wavy swell of coconut trees on precipitous slopes,
The rhythmic sway of blossoms
In the breeze, — night of multi-colored madras
Balanced upon the stems of beautiful bodies!

But what about the "wondrousness" of the tropical mountain? Its malefic aura? Its hard promise? The explosive power of the mountain? Rather than that, swoons, blues, golds, and some pink. That's nice. How overdone! Literature? Yes. Hammock literature. Litera-

ture made of sugar and vanilla. Tourist literature. The Blue Travel
Guide and General Confederation of Labor. Poetry, not in the least.

And I am speaking of Nau! And saying nothing about a Leconte
de l'Isle! About a José Maria de Heredia! About a Francis Jammes.
Colonial professors continue to find that quite good. Poor ninnies!
The "jaguar," le Manchy, the Trophies . . . And this:

> Oh father of my father, you were there standing before
> my soul which had not been born and, under the wind
> the dispatch boats glided into the colonial night

Come on now, real poetry lies elsewhere. Far from rhymes, laments,
sea breezes, parrots. Stiff and stout bamboos changing direction,
we decree the death of sappy, sentimental, folkloric literature. And
to hell with hibiscus, frangipani, and bougainvillea.
Martinican poetry will be cannibal or it will not be.

SUZANNE CÉSAIRE
Tropiques, no. 4, January 1942

The Malaise of a Civilization

If in our legends and short stories, we see suddenly appear a suffering, sensitive, and mocking figure representing our collective self, in ordinary Martinican literary production, we search in vain for the expression of this self.

Why in the past have we been so unconcerned about expressing our ancestral anxiety in a direct manner?

The urgency of this cultural problem escapes only those who are determined to put their hands over their eyes so as not to be disturbed from an artificial peace: and at any cost, even the price of stupidity and death.

As for us, we can feel that our troubling times are going to precipitate the explosion of a ripened fruit, irresistibly called forth by solar fieriness to cast its creative forces to the wind; we can feel on this sun-drenched tranquil land, the formidable, the inescapable pressure of destiny which bathes the entire world in blood in order to give it tomorrow, its new visage.

Let us question life on this island that is ours.

What can we see?

First the geographic position of this strip of land: tropical. Here, we are in the Tropics.

. . . Where the adaptation of an African population has taken place. Imported Blacks had to struggle against the heavy mortality rates of the early stages of slavery, against chronic malnutrition—a reality that persists to this day. And yet one cannot deny that on Martinican soil the colored race produces strong, robust, adaptable men and women of natural elegance and great beauty.

But then, is it not surprising that this people, who over the centuries adapted itself to this land, this authentic Martinican people, is only now beginning to produce authentic works of art? Over the course of the centuries, how is it that there are no viable survivals of the unique styles, for example, of those that flourished so magnificently on African soil? Sculptures, ornate fabrics, paintings, poetry? Let's allow the imbeciles to blame it on the race, on its so-called predisposition to laziness, to thievery, to wickedness.

Let us speak frankly.

If this lack in Black character is not to be explained by the harshness of the tropical climate to which we have adapted, and still less by I don't know what inferiority, it can in fact be explained, believe us, by:

1. the horrific conditions of transplantation onto a foreign soil.

   —We have too soon forgotten the slave ships and the sufferings of our slave forebears. Here forgetfulness is tantamount to cowardice.

2. coerced submission, under pain of the whip and death, to a system of "civilization," to a "style" both even stranger to the new arrivals than the tropical land itself.

3. finally, after the emancipation of people of color, through a collective error concerning our true nature, an error born of this idea, anchored in the deepest part of the popular collective consciousness, from centuries of suffering: "Since the superiority of the colonizers comes to them from a certain life-style, we shall gain strength only by dominating in our turn the technique of this 'style.'"

   Let us stop and measure the far-reaching implications of this gigantic misunderstanding.

■

What is the Martinican fundamentally, intimately, unilaterally? And how does he live?

In providing answers to these questions, we shall see a stunning contradiction appear between the innermost self, with its desires, its impulses, its unconscious forces—and life lived with its necessities, its urgencies, its gravity. A phenomenon of decisive importance for the future of this country.

What is the Martinican?

—A plant-human.

Like a plant, he abandons himself to the rhythm of universal life. There is not the slightest effort to dominate nature. Mediocre farmer. Perhaps. I am not saying that he makes the plant grow: I am saying that he grows, he lives in a plant-like manner. His indolence? that of the vegetal. Do not say "he is lazy," say "he vegetates," and you will speak the truth for two reasons. His favorite phrase: "Let it go." By that, understand that he lets himself be carried along by life, docile, light, un-insistent, non-rebellious—in a friendly way, lovingly. Obstinate moreover as only a plant can be. Independent (independence, autonomy of the plant). Surrender to self, to the seasons, to the moon, to the more-or-less long day. Fruit harvest. And always and everywhere in the slightest manifestations, the primacy of the plant, the plant trampled under foot but still alive, dead but reviving, the plant free, silent, and proud.

Open your eyes—a child is born. To which god should it be entrusted? To the Tree god. Coconut tree or Banana tree, among whose roots the placenta is buried.

Open your ears. According to popular Martinican folklore, the grass that grows on a grave is the living hair of the dead female buried beneath, who is protesting against death. The symbol is always the same: a plant. It is a vital feeling of a life–death community. In short it is the Ethiopian *sentiment of life.**

Consequently the Martinican is typically Ethiopian.** In the depths of his consciousness he is the plant-human, and while iden-

---

* Cf. Frobenius and *Tropiques*, no. 1.

**Another argument could be drawn from architecture: the Martinican hut is an exact reproduction (in contrast to the conical roof, roof in the form of a saddle) of

tifying oneself with the plant, the desire is to abandon oneself to the rhythm of life.

Is this attitude enough to explain his failure in the world?

No—the Martinican has failed because, unaware of his real nature, he tries to lead a life that is not his own. The gigantic phenomenon of a collective lie, of "pseudomorphosis." And the current state of civilization in the West Indies reveals to us the consequences of this mistake.

Repression, sufferings, sterility.

How, why, in this people, only yesterday slaves, can there be this fatal misunderstanding? By the most natural of processes, by the instinct-for-self-preservation game.

Let us remember that what the slave regime prohibited exceedingly, first and foremost, was the assimilation of the Black into the White world. Some decrees: April 30, 1764, prohibited Blacks and coloreds from the practice of medicine; May 9, 1765, forbade the practice of law clerk; and the famous order of February 9, 1779, strictly prohibited Blacks from wearing clothes identical to those of Whites, and required submission and respect for "all Whites in general," etc., etc.

Let us cite further the decree of January 3, 1788, requiring free men of color "to take out permits to work *anywhere other than in the fields.*" One will understand that from that point forward the fundamental goal of the colored man became assimilation. And with overwhelming force, a disastrous confusion takes place in his mind: *liberation means assimilation.*

At the outset it was a good movement: 1848—the mass of freed Blacks, in a sudden outburst of the formative self, refuse all regular work, in spite of the risk of starvation. However, broken by economic necessity, no longer slaves, but wage earners, Blacks will eventually submit to the new discipline of the hoe and the cutlass.

---

the huts of the Beni-Mai people (of the Congo Kasai region), in whom there dominates the "Ethiopian" sentiment of life. Cf. Frobenius, *History of Civilization*, p. 198.

And it is during this period that the repression of the ancestral desire for unrestrained abandon firmly and definitively establishes itself.

It is replaced, especially in the colored middle class, by the unaccustomed desire for competition.

Hence, the drama, evident for those who analyze in depth the collective self of the Martinican people: its unconscious continues to be inhabited by the Ethiopian desire for abandon. However its consciousness, or rather its pre-consciousness, accepts the Hamitic desire for competitiveness. The race for economic fortune, diplomas, unscrupulous social climbing. A struggle shrunken to the standard of being middle class. The pursuit of monkeyshines. Vanity Fair.

The most serious thing is that the desire for imitation—just a short time earlier only a vaguely conscious one since it was a defense mechanism against an oppressive society—has now migrated to the area of fearsome secret forces in the unconscious.

Not one upwardly mobile Martinican will ever admit that he is only engaging in mimicry, so natural, spontaneous, and born of legitimate aspirations does his present situation seem. And, in so doing he will be sincere. He honestly does not KNOW he mimics. He is *unaware* of his true nature, which nonetheless does exist.

In much the same way, *the hysteric* is unaware that he is only *imitating* an illness, but the doctor treating him and curing him of his unhealthy symptoms knows it.

Similarly, the psychoanalyst reveals to us that the effort required of a Martinican in adapting to an unfamiliar life style will not have been without creating a state of pseudo-civilization that one can qualify as *abnormal, of teratoid aberration.*

The current problem is to determine if the Ethiopian attitude that we have discovered as representing the essence itself of the Martinican sentiment of life can be the point of departure for a viable and imposing cultural style.

It is exhilarating to imagine on these tropical shores, finally restored to their inner truth, the long-lasting and fruitful harmony of humankind and soil. Under the sign of plant life.

Here we are called upon to know ourselves finally by ourselves, and here before us are splendors and hopes. Surrealism has given us some of our possibilities. It is up to us to find the others. With its guiding light.

And let me be clear:

It is not at all about a backwards return, a resurrection of an African past that we have learned to know and respect. On the contrary, it is about the mobilization of every living strength brought together upon this earth where race is the result of the most unremitting intermixing; it is about becoming conscious of the incredible store of varied energies until now locked up within us. We must now deploy them to the maximum without deviation, without falsification. Too bad for those who consider us mere dreamers.

The most unsettling reality is our own.

We shall act.

This land, ours, can only be what we want it to be.

SUZANNE CÉSAIRE
Tropiques, no. 5, April 1942

1943
Surrealism and Us

the river of grass snakes that I call my veins
the river of battlements that I call my blood
the river of bantu spears that I call my face
the river trekking on foot around the world
will strike the Artesian rock with one hundred monsoon stars

Liberty my only pirate water of the new year my only thirst
love my only sampan boat
we shall slip our fingers of laughter and calabash
between the icy teeth of the Sleeping Beauty in the woods

Many have believed that surrealism was dead. Many wrote so. Childish nonsense: its activity extends today to the entire world and surrealism remains livelier, more audacious than ever. André Breton can look with pride upon the period between the wars and affirm that the mode of expression he created more than twenty years ago is opening upon an increasingly vast and immense "beyond."

If the whole world is struck by the influence of French poetry at a time when the most horrible disaster in its history swoops down upon France, it is, in part, because the great voice of André Breton was not stilled, and that is because everywhere, in New York, in Brazil, in Mexico, in Argentina, in Cuba, in Canada, in Algiers, voices echo that would not be what they are (in timber and resonance) without surrealism. Actually, today as twenty years ago, surrealism can claim the glory of being at the extreme point of the bow of life drawn to the breaking point.

The presence therefore of surrealism. Young, ardent, and revolutionary. Most certainly, in 1943, surrealism remains what it has always been, an activity which assigns itself the goal of exploring and expressing systematically the forbidden zones of the human mind, in order to neutralize them: an activity which desperately seeks to give humankind the means of reducing the ancient antinomies that are "the true alembics of suffering"; a power, the only one, that allows us to reconnect with "this original, unique faculty, that the primitive and the child still retain traces of, that lifts the spell of the impassable barrier between the inner world and the outer world." But as the surrealist cause in art, as in life, is the cause itself of freedom, the sign itself of vitality, surrealism has itself evolved. Evolution, better yet, a blossoming outward in all directions. When Breton created surrealism, the most urgent task was to free the mind from the shackles of absurd logic and so-called Western reason.

But when freedom found itself threatened throughout the world in 1943, surrealism, which never for a single instant ceased to stand in service to the greatest emancipation of humankind, wanted to sum up the entirety of all its efforts in one magical word: freedom.

In art as in life, the surrealist cause is the cause itself of freedom. Today more than ever, to draw one's inspiration abstractly from freedom, or to celebrate it in conventional terms, is to do it a disservice. In order to enlighten the world, freedom must make itself flesh and blood and, toward that end, must be reflected and recreated in language, in the word.

Thus speaks Breton. The demand for freedom. The necessity of absolute purity—it's the Saint-Just side of Breton, hence his "Thank you, but no" to concessions, harshly denounced by his friends more given to compromise.

To those who ask periodically why certain schisms have occurred at the center of the surrealist movement, why such abrupt exclusions have been pronounced, I believe I can reply in all clear conscience that those who eliminated themselves in the process had, in some more or less obvious way, broken a solemn pact with freedom, freedom being revered in its pure state by surrealists — that is to say, advocated in all its forms — there are, of course, many ways to have broken this pact. In my opinion, it was, for example, to have returned, as did some former surrealists, to fixed forms in poetry, when it has been demonstrated, particularly in the French language — the exceptional influence of French poetry since Romanticism allows me to generalize in this way — that the quality of lyric expression has benefitted from nothing so much as the will to be emancipated from obsolete rules: Rimbaud, Lautréamont mute things, the Mallarmé of "A Throw of the Dice," the most important symbolists (Maeterlinck, Saint-Pol-Roux), Apollinaire's "conversation-poems." And this would be just as true for painting during the same period. In place of the preceding names, it would suffice to cite those of Van Gogh, Seurat, Rousseau, Matisse, Picasso, Duchamp. It was also a betrayal, once and for all, of the freedom to renounce personal expression" and in that way even dangerously always outside the strict frameworks to which a "party" wants to restrain you, even were it in your eyes the party of freedom (loss of the feeling of uniqueness). Freedom is at once madly desirable and quite fragile, which gives it the right to be jealous.

The intransigence consequently of freedom, which is, moreover, itself the condition of its fruitfulness. And we see that Breton, at the end of his most moving examinations, does not hesitate to venture into the most wide-ranging virginal spaces that surrealism has yielded to human daring. What does Breton ask of the most insightful minds of the period? Nothing less than the courage to embark upon an adventure which may prove deadly, from all one can tell, but which one may hope — and that is the essence — will lead to the total conquest of the mind. "A period, like the one we live in, can manage, if it has as a goal the arousal of mistrust for all the conventional ways of thinking the insufficiency of which is only too obvious, for travels à la Bergerac and Gulliver. And, not excluded from the voyage on which I invite you today, is every possibility of arriv-

ing somewhere, even after certain detours, to lands more reason-
able than the one we leave behind." Surrealism is living, intensely,
magnificently, having found and perfected a method of inquiry of
immeasurable efficacy. The dynamism of surrealism. And it is this
sense of movement that has kept it always in the avant-garde, infinitely sensitive to the disruptions of the period, the "scourge of
balance."

Such is surrealist activity, a total activity, the only one that can
liberate humankind by revealing to it the unconscious, one of the
activities that will aid in liberating people by illuminating the blind
myths that have led them to this point.

■

And now, a return to ourselves.

We know where we stand in Martinique. The arrow of history
dizzyingly indicated for us our human task: a society, corrupt from
its origins through crime, reliant for the present on injustice and
hypocrisy, fearful of its future because of its guilty conscience,
must morally, historically, and inevitably disappear.

From among the powerful war weaponry the modern world now
places at our disposal, our audacity has chosen surrealism, which
offers the greatest chances for success.

Already one result is established. At no moment during these
difficult years of Vichy domination was the image of freedom ever
totally extinguished here, and we owe this to surrealism. We are
happy to have sustained this image in the eyes even of those who
thought they had destroyed it forever. Blind because they were
ignorant, they failed to see it laughing insolently, aggressively, in
our pages. Cowards later, when they did understand, fearful and
ashamed.

So, far from contradicting, diminishing, or diverting our revolutionary feeling for life, surrealism shored it up. It nourished in us
an impatient strength, endlessly sustaining this massive army of
negations.

And then I think also to tomorrow.

Millions of Black hands, across the raging clouds of world war, will spread terror everywhere. Roused from a long benumbing torpor, this most deprived of all people will rise up, upon plains of ashes.

Our surrealism will then supply them the leaven from their very depths. It will be time finally to transcend the sordid contemporary antinomies: Whites–Blacks, Europeans–Africans, civilized–savage: the powerful magic of the mahoulis will be recovered, drawn from the very wellsprings of life. Colonial idiocies will be purified by the welding arc's blue flame. The mettle of our metal, our cutting edge of steel, our unique communions—all will be recovered.

■

Surrealism, tightrope of our hope.

SUZANNE CÉSAIRE
Tropiques, nos. 8–9, October 1943

The Great Camouflage

There are, melded into the isles, beautiful green waves of water and of silence. There is the purity of sea salt all around the Caribbean. There is before my eyes, the pretty square in Pétionvile, planted with pines and hibiscus. There is my island, Martinique, and its fresh necklace of clouds buffeted by Mount Pélé. There are the highest plateaus of Haiti, where a horse dies, lightning-struck by the age-old killer storm at Hinche. Next to it, his master contemplates the land he believed sound and expansive. He does not yet know that he is participating in the island's absence of equilibrium. But this sudden access to terrestrial madness illuminates his heart: he begins to think about the other Caribbean islands, their volcanoes, their earthquakes, their hurricanes.

At this moment off the coast of Puerto Rico a huge cyclone begins to spin its way between the seas of clouds, with its beautiful tail sweeping rhythmically the semi-circle of the Antilles. The Atlantic takes flight toward Europe with great oceanic waves. Our little tropical observatories begin to crackle with the news. The Wireless Telegraph Services go crazy. The boats flee, but to where? The sea swells, here, there, with a delicious bound, the sea stretches its limbs for a greater consciousness of its elemental water power, faces dripping, sailors grit their teeth, and we learn that the southeast coast of the Haitian Republic is in the path of the cyclone passing at a speed of thirty-five miles per hour, making its way toward Florida. Consternation seizes objects and the people spared at the fringes of the wind. Do not move. Let it pass . . .

At the center of the cyclone everything cracks, everything collapses in the ripping sound of great manifestations. Then the radios go silent. The great line of palm trees of cool wind unfurled somewhere in the stratosphere, there where no one will go to follow incredible iridescences and waves of violet light.

After the rain, the sun.

The Haitian cicadas are thinking of screeching love. When there is no longer a drop of water in the burnt grass, they sing furiously that life is beautiful, they explode in a cry too vibrant for an insect body. Their thin film of dried silk stretched to the breaking point, they die while letting surge forth the least moist scream of pleasure on earth.

Haiti goes on, enveloped in the ashes of the sun sweet to the eyes of the cicadas, with scales of the *mabouyas*, with the metallic face of the sea that is no longer of water but of mercury.

Now is the moment to look out the window of the aluminum clipper with its great banking turns.

Once again the sea of clouds is no longer virginal since the Pan American Airways System planes have been flying through. If there is a harvest maturing, now is the time to try to glimpse it, but in the prohibited military zones, the windows are closed.

On the planes they bring forth the disinfectants, or the ozone, whatever, you will see nothing. Nothing but the sea and the indistinct outline of lands. One can only guess the easy lovemaking of fish. They make the water move and wink amicably for the aircraft's porthole. Our islands seen from above, take on their true dimension as seashells. And as for the hummingbird-women, tropical flower-women, the women of four races and dozens of bloodlines, they are there no longer. Neither the heliconia, nor the frangipani, nor the flame tree, nor the palm trees in the moonlight, nor the sunsets unlike any other in the world . . .

Yet they are there.

Yet fifteen years ago, a revelation of the Antilles, from the eastern flank of Mount Pélé. From that point on, I knew, very young, that Martinique was sensual, coiled upon itself, stretched out, unwound in the Caribbean, and I suddenly thought about the other islands which are so beautiful.

Once again in Haiti, during the summer mornings of '44, the presence of the Antilles, more than perceptible, from places in which, like Kenscoff, the view over the mountains is unbearably beautiful.

And now total insight. My gaze, over and beyond these shapes and these perfect colors, catches, upon the very beautiful Antillean face, its inner torments.

For the pattern of unfulfilled desires has trapped the Antilles and America. From the time of the arrival of the conquistadors and the rise of their technical know how (beginning with firearms), the lands from across the Atlantic have changed, not only in facial appearance but in fear. Fear of being surpassed by those who remained in Europe, already armed and equipped, fear of being in competition with people of color quickly declared inferior in order to better beat them down. It was necessary first and at all costs, be it even the price of the Black slave trade's infamy, to re-create an American society richer, more powerful, better organized than the European society left behind—yet still desired. It was necessary to take this revenge upon the nostalgic hell that was vomiting its adventurer demons, its galley slaves, its penitents, its utopians upon the shores of the New World and its islands. For three centuries, colonial adventurism has continued—the wars of independence are only an episode—and the American people, whose behavior vis-à-vis Europe has remained often childish and romantic, are still not freed from the grip of the old continent. Of course it is the Blacks of the Americas who suffer the most, in a daily humiliation, from the degradations, the injustices, and the pettiness of colonial society.

If we are proud to observe everywhere on American soil our extraordinary vitality, if definitively this vitality seems to hold out the promise of our salvation, one must, however, dare to say that refined forms of slavery still run rampant. Here, in these French islands, they debase the thousands of Blacks for whom a century ago the great Schœlcher sought, along with freedom and dignity, the title of citizen. Since many among the French seem determined to tolerate not even the slightest shadow being cast upon that visage, one must dare show, on the face of France, illuminated with the implacable light of events, the Antillean stain.

The degrading forms of the modern wage-system continue to find in our homeland a ground on which to flourish without constraint.

There the system will dump, along with outmoded material from their factories, these few thousands of second-rate manufacturers and grocers, this caste of would-be colonizers responsible for the human deprivation of the Antilles.

Released onto the streets of their capitals, an insurmountable timidity fills them with fear among their European brothers. Ashamed of their drawling accent, of their unrefined French, they sigh longingly for the peaceful warmth of Antillean houses and the patois of the Black "nanny" of their childhood.

Quite prepared to engage in all types of betrayals in order to defend themselves against the constantly rising tide of Blacks, if the Americans had not just claimed that the purity of their blood was more than suspect, these same people would have sold themselves to America, as they had during the '40s when they declared loyalty to the Vichy admiral: Pétain being for them the sacrificial altar of France, thus Admiral Robert necessarily became "the tabernacle of the Antilles."

In the meantime the Antillean serf lives miserably, abjectly on the lands of "the factory," and the mediocrity of our townships is a nauseating spectacle. In the meantime the Antilles continues to be paradise, this soft rustling of palms . . .

Irony that day was a shining vestment full of sparks, each one of our muscles was expressing in a personal manner a fragment of desire scattered among the mango trees in blossom.

I was listening very attentively, without being able to hear your voices lost in the Caribbean symphony that was launching whirlwinds of water against the islands. We were like thoroughbreds, restrained, pawing the ground with impatience, at the edge of this salt savannah.

On the beach there were some "metropolitan functionaries." They were landed there, without conviction, ready to take off at the first signal. The new arrivals are hardly adapting to our "old French territories." When they lean over the malefic mirror of the Caribbean, they see therein the delirious reflection of themselves. They dare not recognize themselves in this ambiguous being, the Antillean. They know that the *métis* have a part of their blood, that they are, like them, of Western civilization. Of course it is understood that the "metropolitans" are unaware of the prejudice of color. But colored descendants fill them with fear, in spite of the smiles exchanged. They were not expecting this strange bourgeoning of their blood. Perhaps they would like not to respond to the Antillean heir who shouts, but does not shout out "my father." However one will have to deal with these unanticipated boys, these charming girls. One must govern these unruly people.

Here is an Antillean, great-grandson of a White colonizer and a slave Negress. Here he is deploying, in order "to get up and running" in his island, all the energies formerly necessary to greedy colonizers for whom the blood of others was the natural price of gold, all the courage necessary to African warriors who perpetually earned their living from death.

Here he is with his double strength and double ferocity, in a dangerously threatened equilibrium: he cannot accept his negritude; he cannot whiten himself. Spinelessness takes hold of this divided heart. And, with it, the usual trickery, the taste for "schemes"; thus blossoms in the Antilles this flower of human baseness, the colored bourgeoisie.

On the roads bordered with glyciridia, delightful little black kids, ecstatically digesting the roots cooked with or without salt, smile at the luxury automobile passing by. They feel abruptly, deep in their navel, the need one day to be the masters of a beast equally as supple, shiny, and powerful. Years later, dirtied with the garage grease of happiness, one sees them miraculously give the spark of life to junkyard wrecks, disposed of at a very low price. By instinct, the hands of thousands of young Antilleans have weighed steel, found joints, loosened screws. Thousands of images of gleaming factories, virgin steel, liberating machines, have filled the hearts of our young workers. There is, in hundreds of squalid warehouses where scrap iron rusts, an invisible vegetation of desires. The impatient fruits of revolution will spring up from it, inevitably.

Here, between the wind-smoothed mountains is Free-Peoples-Estates. A peasant who himself was not swept up in the hoopla surrounding the mechanical adventure, leaned against the great Mapou tree of spirits that shades an entire side of the mountain, and felt rising within himself, through his toes dug firmly into the mud, a slow vegetal up-thrust. He turned toward the sunset to discern the next day's weather—the orangey reds indicated to him that planting time was approaching—his gaze is not just the peaceful reflection of the light, for it grows heavy with impatience, the same kind that stirs up the land of Martinique, his land that does not belong to him yet is however his land. He knows that it is with them, the workers, that the land has a shared and common cause, and not with the colonial Whites or the mulattoes. And when, abruptly, in the Caribbean night, all decked out in love and quiet, there bursts forth the call of drums, the Blacks ready themselves to respond to the desire of the earth and of the dance, but the landowners lock themselves up in their mansions, and behind their metallic spider-web curtains, they are, under the electric light, so like pale and entrapped moths.

Around them the tropical night swells with rhythms, Bergilde's hips have taken their cataclysmic speed from the heaving rising from the depths to the flanks of the volcanoes, and it is Africa herself who, from across the Atlantic and the centuries pre-dating the slave-ships, dedicates to her Antillean children the gaze of sun-filled desire that the dancers exchange. Their cry exclaims in a husky and full voice that Africa is still there, present, that she waits, undulating, devourer of Whites, immensely virgin in spite of colonization. And upon the faces constantly bathed in marine effluvia close to the islands, on these small restricted lands surrounded by water, like great impassable gulfs, the tremendous wind passes by, come from a continent. Antilles-Africa, thanks to the drums, the nostalgia for earthly spaces lives on in the hearts of these islanders. Who will overcome this nostalgia?

The heliconia shrubs and flowers of Absalon Forest bleed over the chasms, and the beauty of the tropical landscape goes to the heads of the poets passing by. Across the swaying latticed networks of the palms they can see the Antillean conflagration rolling across the Caribbean that is a tranquil sea of lavas. Here life lights up in a vegetal fire. Here, on these hot lands that keep alive geological species, the fixed plant, passion and blood, in its primitive architecture, the disquieting ringing suddenly issue from the chaotic backs of the dancers. Here the tropical vines rocking vertiginously, take on ethereal poses to charm the precipices, with their trembling fingertips they latch onto the ungraspable cosmic flurry rising all throughout the drum-filled nights. Here the poets feel their heads capsize, and inhaling the fresh smells of the ravines, they take possession of the wreath of the islands, they listen to the sound of the water surrounding the islands, and they see tropical flames kindled no longer in the heliconia, in the gerberas, in the hibiscus, in the bougainvilleas, in the flame trees, but instead in the hungers, and in the fears, in the hatreds, in the ferocity, that burn in the hollows of the mountains.

It is thus that the Caribbean conflagration blows its silent fumes, blinding for the only eyes that know how to see, and suddenly the blues of the Haitian mountains, of the Martinican bays, turn dull, suddenly the most blazing reds go pale, and the sun is no longer a crystal play of light, and if the public squares have chosen the laceworks of Jerusalem thorn as luxury fans against the fieriness of the sky, if the flowers have known how to find just the right colors to leave one dumbstruck, if the tree-like ferns have secreted golden saps for their white crooks, rolled-up like a sex organ, if my Antilles are so beautiful, it is because the great game of hide-and-seek has succeeded, it is then because, on that day, the weather is most certainly too blindingly bright and beautiful to see clearly therein.

SUZANNE CÉSAIRE
Tropiques, nos. 13–14, 1945

Part Two

FOR MADAME SUZANNE CÉSAIRE

Then bells rang out to the four corners of the school,
accompanied by the cheerful laughter of little *chabine* girls,
with hair often lighter than their complexion. One searches,
among these native essences, by what wood this beautiful
flesh of prismatic shadow is warmed: coconut, coffee, vanilla
whose printed foliages with a persistent mystery adorn the
paper of the coffee bags in which will nestle the unknown
desire of childhood. With what ultimate mixture in mind,
what enduring balance between day and night—as one dreams
of retaining the exact second when, during very calm times,
the sun in sinking into the sea realizes the phenomenon
of the "green diamond"—this search, at the bottom of the
crucible, for feminine beauty so very often far more exquisitely
accomplished here than elsewhere and which has never
appeared to me more dazzling than in a face of white ash and
embers.

ANDRÉ BRETON, August 1941
Tropiques, no. 3, October 1941

The Creole Dialogue

Like Columbus who would discover the West Indies,
believing himself en route to the East Indies,
in the twentieth century the painter found himself
in the presence of a new world before having become
suddenly aware that he could exit the old.
— ANDRÉ BRETON, *Surrealism and Painting*, Gallimard, 1965

Fleeing the old world of Europe collapsed under triumphant Nazism, an overcrowded cargo of exiles headed toward America made a stopover for a month in Fort-de-France en route to New York, which occasioned the event that was the meeting of Aimé and Suzanne Césaire and their *Tropiques* friends, with principally the Cuban painter Wifredo Lam, his wife Helena, André Breton, his wife the artist Jacqueline Lamba, and also with André Masson and his family, Claude Levi-Strauss, and Anna Seghers. The role that this layover in Martinique has had in literary and artistic history is significant. It is there that Breton discovered the first issue of the revue *Tropiques*, while buying a ribbon for his daughter Aube in a notions shop, and the text of *Notebook of a Return to the Native Land* in the unique version of the little revue *Volontés*—a dazzling discovery according to him of the "greatest lyrical monument of that time," for which he will preface the first edition in France published by Bordas in 1947, illustrated with a painting by Lam. It was also for the Césaire couple "love at first sight" between Lam and themselves, and the birth of a binding literary friendship with Breton. Numerous exchanges were to take place between them, despite the obstacles placed before them by the Pétain government authorities and police. The high point of this meeting was an excursion where the Césaires led their new friends out into the middle of nature in the Absalon forest, one of the places of strength and inspiration for the thinking of Suzanne and Aimé Césaire. It proved to be an excursion of extraordinarily fertile artistic consequence, since it marked the origin of an evolution in Lam's work, illustrated by his masterpiece *The Jungle*, 1943, and the origin of the Breton book, *Martinique: Snake Charmer*, and of the finale of the last text of Suzanne Césaire: "The Great Camouflage," in direct echo of the "Creole Dialogue" between Masson and Breton, this being why this dialogue is partially reproduced here, with some poems by André Breton, André Masson, and René Ménil, inspired quite particularly by the person and thought of Suzanne Césaire.

DANIEL MAXIMIM

Antille

At night the house fires gaze at themselves in the reflection of
the land's glance. A grand ballet of palms, set in place by silence,
motionless, rustles in the fresh dancing air.

∎

Crested with bamboo groves my wild mountain head collides
with a dream of a nude in the clouds and sees, diving from a
maelstrom of foliage—hovering in its flight—the hummingbird.

∎

Arborescent fur of eviscerated earth fan of desire surge of sap
yes it is the fan of heavy leaf in fruited air. Question the sensitive
one it answers no but in the heart of the vaginal shade, red reigns,
carnal flower of the heliconia—blood congealed in the remarkable
flower. Spermatic lava it nourished you shaping the common
glass the hand of the fire made it shimmer with mortal mother of
pearl. The great hand caresses the breast of the mountain unless
it caresses your rump Anthracite Venus it rustles the fringe of
the palms lifts the feathery fronds and slides under the amorous
fleece of an enormous Sylvan landscape.

∎

In the sky of your forehead the cry of the flame tree
On the turf of your lips the pulled-out tongue of the hibiscus
In the hot countryside of your belly the cane fields in a crown
    of flavor
In the verdant openings your firefly eyes
At your breasts the fine mango
The breadfruit tree for all your people
And the manchineel tree for the hooded beast.

ANDRÉ MASSON
In André Breton's *Martinique: Snake Charmer*
Sagittaire edition, 1948

The Creole Dialogue
between André Breton and André Masson

[. . .]

—The forest envelops us; it has its magical charms, we were familiar with them before coming here. Do you recall a drawing I entitled "Vegetal delirium"? That delirium is there, in the forest, we can touch it, we can participate in it. We are one of these trees several stories high, bearing in miniature in the hollowed-out part of its branches a swamp with all of its parasitic vegetation grafted onto its central trunk: rising, falling, active, passive, and draped from top to bottom in jungle vines with star-shaped flowers.

—You find yourself in there like no other. Everything has remained in place for so long. One will end up perceiving that surrealist landscapes are not so arbitrary. It is inevitable that they find their resolution in these lands where nature has in no way been dominated. What a Rimbaud dream it is of foregrounds and backgrounds in dramatic counterpoint like this waterfall onto a valley at the bottom of which growls the musical instrument of all whirlpools.

—Yes, everything is out there in the world, and I know nothing more laughable as the fear of the imagination that can fetter the painter. Nature and its profusion put him to shame:

To find flowers that are chairs!

But it takes so little to have them right before our eyes!

—One can wonder to what extent the poverty of European vegetation is responsible for the flight of the mind toward an imaginary flora. That from which one wants to escape today, is it from what we see in general or only what we see in particular from the assault upon our senses when we find ourselves in impoverished places? Some, in a deliberate way, have left Europe solely for this reason. It is striking to think that Gauguin passed through Martinique and contemplated settling there.

—Exoticism, one will say on the negative side, exoticism, there the forbidden word is pronounced. But what is to be understood by exoticism? The entire earth belongs to us. My birth within proximity to a weeping willow tree is not a reason for devoting my artistic expression to this somewhat short attachment.

—Wherever we are condemned to live, we are not, however, totally limited to the landscape outside our window: there are the illustrations from childhood books, from which so many visual memories are drawn, hardly less real than others. But here the need for something other is, all the same, not as great as elsewhere; do you not find that so? One has truly nothing to add to this setting in order to perfect it. I don't dream, of course, of rehabilitating the art of imitation, but it would appear to me less reprehensible here than elsewhere.

—The reprehensible, to my mind, is to impoverish that which exists. Quite young, we dreamed in front of Picturesque Store and later we loved the jungles of douanier Rousseau that you, I believe, have found in Mexico.

—Here Rousseau is more at home than over there. You know that people frequently question whether he actually saw America with his own eyes. There, in my opinion, is a problem of the greatest importance, [. . .] Even if Rousseau had not budged from France, one would have to admit that his psychology of the primitive afforded him the discovery of entire primitive spaces consonant with reality. There would appear to exist therefore, beyond the obstacles posed by civilization, a mysterious communication, secondary, always possible between men on the basis of what united them originally, and divided them. That would be a more deserving explanation than the empty observation to which one is limited on this topic.

[. . .]

—We think we can abandon ourselves with impunity to the forest and there, all of a sudden, its twists and turns obsess us: shall we ever get out of this green labyrinth, shall we not be at the Panic Gates?

—By a stroke of good fortune we shall not have to search very far for the antidote. Without falling into the finalism of *Paul and Virginia*, one delights in the idea that the southern part of the island contradicts and conjures up the perilous dimensions of the landscape.

—I see the guarantee itself of a deliverance. Yes we were smitten by the vegetal force, and yet the compelling need we experienced to maintain regular forms in a place of nature where precisely the seemingly unpredictable, I mean the lack of a framework, seems predominant. What is more revealing?

—Let's carry off symbolically the heliconia flower beautiful as the circulation of blood from the lowest to the highest of the species, the chalices filled to the brim with this marvelous sediment. That it be the heraldic end of the conciliation we seek between the perceptible and the boundless, life and dream—it is through an elaborate gate that we shall pass in order to continue to advance in the only valid way that is: through the fire.

From André Breton's *Martinique: Snake Charmer*
Sagittaire edition, 1948

Let Poetry Go

[. . .] But, colonial friend, I assure you and do believe me, I like you, charming character, for once again, I really want to lift the corner of the veil for you, just for one tiny second. But be careful that your sugary sweetened stomach does not heave in front of a scene prepared for a spectator other than yourself. You will come to understand just how many oceans separate us . . . A forest, next to Mount Pélée. The sun at this close of the day (you would not be able to endure the devouring light of midday) lights its campfire at the base of tree trunks sleek and no doubt sonorous. Sometimes the light comes forth in waves of fiery glimmers, sometimes, quietly, takes over the forest with an aborted light, yellow and infinitely subtle. At this moment one can hear, come from afar, from behind the trees that are moving, that are not moving, this melody, alternately muted and blaring, of Duke Ellington, the marvelous *Mood Indigo*. A sudden anxiety grips your heart and you turn your head sharply to the left, *expecting the worst*. In a clearing, up until then unnoticed, you glimpse a scene of prodigious beauty. Bathed in a living–dying reddish-yellow light and bathed also it seems in great ellingtonian chords, there a Caribbean grander than life amorously devours the enthralling object of its love . . .

Your heart, my dear colonial hare, cannot get used to this sublime spectacle, you feel that your presence is incongruous and you leave, silently, embarrassed, on tiptoe, by an opportune path.

And in the forest there lingers this exalting image of absolute love that before our eyes, the pure child eater of toys and sometimes lovers boldly realize . . .

■

Get over not liking poetry.
One never loves that which does not deserve to be loved.

■

. . . Beautiful as the encounter in the Antillean forest at the center of a clearing illuminated by the subtle bleeding light, of a cannibal and of woman of ash pale complexion.

■

A literature is taking shape.

What we do not worry about is whether it pleases you or not. Who does not see that, for this literature, it would not be a propitious sign if it were pleasing to you, to your shadow ever-adorned in clouds of disinvolvement? Martinican poetry will be cannibalistic. Or it will not be.

RENÉ MÉNIL
Tropiques, no. 5, April 1942

Part Three

Windows of the swamp flower ah! flower
Upon the heavy silence of the night for Suzanne Césaire
from sonorous butterflies
Friend
We shall spread our oceanic sails,
Toward the lost surge of the pampas and the rocks
And we shall sing to the low tides
        inexhaustibly the song of the rising dawn.

AIMÉ CÉSAIRE
"Just to Live, A Narrative," *Tropiques*, no. 4, January 1942

Aimé-Suzy

[. . .] woman is less submissive to the tyranny of logic because she is more faithful to the cosmos; she has less method because she has more nostalgia; woman (the memory of the species) has preserved intact the memory of the marvelous dramatic shifts that have punctuated humanity's first experiences, memory of the time when the sun was young and the earth was supple, and all things considered, what one calls the "irrealism" of woman is only the will to return to thinking its irrational force, of course, its aberrant force, I concede, but also its force of forward thrust, creation, and of renewal [. . .]

It pleases me to invoke the revolutionary phrase of Rimbaud, this sentence so very wise and seminal that I excerpt from one of the most resonant hymns that has ever been written in praise of the creative faculty and this is nothing other than Rimbaud's famous letter to Paul Demeny.

"When the endless servitude of woman is broken, when she will live for and by herself, man—heretofore abominable—having given her release to her, she herself too will be a poet! Woman will find some of the unknown! She will find strange things. We shall take them. We shall understand them."

[. . .]

And now, young ladies, you understand that I was not wrong a short while ago when I said that we share a common cause and that we are liable to the same justice, that before the world's tribunal we are held to the same responsibilities, and that in the great outline of the universal project of humankind, we are held to the same qualifications.

AIMÉ CÉSAIRE, speech at the awards ceremony
of the Fort de France Colonial Boarding School for Girls,
June 1945

In the pages that follow we present some of Aimé Césaire's poems that are dedicated to Suzanne Césaire. The great literary fruitfulness born of their union from the time of their meeting in Paris through these years of their revue *Tropiques* is evident, just like the evidence of their great love and their poetic complicity. At the end of his life, Aimé Césaire confided "we breathed together with faith in the future." All throughout his theatrical and poetic work the strength of their union shines through, the fears for her fragile health, the drama of their separation at Suzanne's request, the family void and the solitude after her death, the persistence in him of the memory of fertile complicity, and this traceable up until his very last poems:

> Through the cicatricial opening-closing games of the sky
> I can see her fluttering her eyelids
> Just to let me know that she understands my signals
> Which are moreover in distress from very old sun-falls of light
> Hers I truly believe to be the only one capable of capturing
>   them still . . .

DANIEL MAXIMIN

Hair

Ingenuous flames you who lick a rare heart
the forest will remember the water and the alburnum
as I too remember the tender muzzle
of big rivers stumbling around like blind men
the forest remembers that the last word can only be
the flaming cry of the bird from the ruins in the bowl of the
      storm

Innocent one who goes there
forget to remember that
the baobab is our tree
it barely waves arms so dwarfed
one would almost say it is an imbecilic giant
and you
dwelling place of my insolence my tombs my torrents
shock of hair wave of tropical vines fervent hope of
      shipwrecked souls
sleep softly by the meticulous trunk of my embrace my
woman
my citadel

AIMÉ CÉSAIRE, *Cadastre*

Seismic Shift

So many great patches of dreams
So many intimate parts of homelands
        collapsed
fallen empty and the sullied sonorous foaming wake of the idea
and the two of us? what two of us?
More or less the old story of the family surviving the disaster
"in the old snake in the garden smell of our bloods we were
        fleeing
the valley, the village pursuing us with its roaring stone lions
        on our heels."
Sleep, restless sleep, bad awakening of the heart
Yours over mine cracked dishes piled up in the pitching trough
        of meridians
To try words? Their friction in order to conjure the unformed as
        nocturnal insects rub their elytrons of madness?
Caught, caught, caught outside the lie caught
caught caught caught
        beaten down pushed headlong
        according to nothing

other than the poorly read abrupt persistence
of our true names, our miraculous names
until now lodging in the storehouse of
forgetfulness.

AIMÉ CÉSAIRE, *Ferrements*

Son of Thunder and Lightning

And without her ever deigning to seduce the jailers
at her bosom a bouquet of hummingbirds breaks up
at her ears buds of atolls shoot up
she speaks to me a language so soft that at first I do not comprehend but eventually I grasp that she is assuring me
that Spring has come against the current
that every thirst is quenched that we are in Autumn's good graces
that the stars in the street have blossomed at high noon and
hang their fruits very low

AIMÉ CÉSAIRE, *Cadastre*

Suzanne Césaire, My Mother

My mother,
Beautiful as the flame of her thought,
My mother with eyes the color of amber and a luminous expression
with the light skin of a golden *chabine*, with the long graceful silhouette,
with the electric hair that she loved to undo to amuse us,
we, her children, before sliding her metal comb through it to make sparks fly.
My mother with the long slender fingers of a pianist *sans* piano,
Letting disappear between her tapering fingers
The blue smoke from her banned English cigarette.
At the time no other mother smoked
and no other mother read Chekhov with her morning coffee
. . .
My mother, as elegant in her simple blue Tricosa outfit as though she were wearing a tailored suit by Chanel.
"I can wear any old thing!" she used to say laughing.
My mother, sitting down, at nightfall, near our beds,
Villa Week-End, in Petit Clamart,
to tell us the eternal story,
The one about Koulivikou, which had no ending
and for which she invented the next installment each evening
. . .
My militant mother hungry for freedom
sensitive to the sufferings of the oppressed
unwilling to accept any injustices
enamored of literature and passionate about history,
making us be quiet when our father was working,
writing tirelessly, with her mysterious script,
on white sheets with the letterhead of the National Assembly.

My mother, esteemed teacher, although for a long time nicknamed
"the Black Panther" by some of her students,
spending all of her evenings correcting papers,
often embellished with pictures by the youngest of us.
About which, far from scolding us, she was quite amused.
My mother active feminist *avant la lettre*
alert to every stage of women's liberation,
"Yours will be the generation of women with choices"
she said to me one day.
Little by little, the marvelous short stories were replaced by real narratives,
often more cruel, come from Martinique and elsewhere.
I was nine at the time of the Bordeaux trial of the Basse-Pointe Sixteen.
I was eleven and I cried at the time of the execution of Julius and Ethel Rosenberg.
I was fourteen and I cried at the time of the assassination of Emmett Till
who, at the time of his death, was only a year older than I.
They were my first political revolts.
My mother who believed more in struggles than in tears,
My mother with the explosive humor,
with the gaiety tinged with melancholy,
with fragile health, but indefatigable tenacity.
My unforgettable mother, who was not able to grow old,
Suzanne Césaire, born Roussi.
Maman Suzy. That is what we used to call her.

INA CÉSAIRE
January 2009

Contributors

In 1941, SUZANNE CÉSAIRE cofounded the journal *Tropiques*, which dealt with surrealism and black culture in African-Caribbean literature. She wrote numerous essays for the journal denouncing colonialism and cultural alienations. She is also the author of the plays *Auroré de le liberté* and *Youma, Dawn of Freedom*, a lost manuscript.

KEITH L. WALKER is professor of French and Francophone studies at Dartmouth College. A literary critic and translator, he is the author of many publications, including *Countermodernism and Francophone Literary Culture: The Game of Slipknot* (Duke 1999).

ANDRÉ MASSON (1896–1987) was a French artist known for his interest in surrealism and his use of automatic drawing, as well as his graphic depictions of the Spanish Civil War.

ANDRÉ BRETON (1896–1966) was as French writer and poet, best known as the founder of surrealism. His writings include the first *Surrealist Manifesto*, in which he defines the movement as "pure psychic automatism."

RENÉ MÉNIL (1907–2004), a French surrealist writer and philosopher, lived on the island of Martinique. He began the Antillanité movement, which stresses the creation of a specific West Indian identity out of a multiplicity of ethnic and cultural elements.

AIMÉ FERNAND DAVID CÉSAIRE (1913–2008) was a French poet, playwright, essayist, and politician from Martinique. He was one of the founders of the Négritude movement in Francophone literature.